QC
16
.E5
I74
1989

Ireland, Karin.

Albert Einstein.

$13.98

Albert
Einstein

PIONEERS in CHANGE

Albert
Einstein

KARIN IRELAND

Silver Burdett Press
Englewood Cliffs, New Jersey

This book is dedicated to a very special person,
Tricia, with much love.

I'd like to thank Eric Christian at Caltech
for helping me explain the physics work Einstein did.

PHOTOGRAPH ACKNOWLEDGMENTS:
AP/Wide World Photos: frontispiece, 43, 50–51, 58, 68–69, 74, 80, 83, 86–87, 96; Culver Pictures, Inc.: 57; Frederic Lewis/Lass: 84; The Hewbrew University of Jerusalem, Courtesy, American Institute of Physics, Niels Bohr Library: 8, 35, 20 Gift of Helmut Drubber; Lotte Jacobi Collection: 3.

SERIES AND COVER DESIGN:
R STUDIO T • Raúl Rodríguez and Rebecca Tachna

ART DIRECTOR:
Carol Kuchta

MANAGING EDITOR
Nancy Furstinger

PROJECT EDITOR:
Richard G. Gallin

PHOTO RESEARCH:
Lenore Weber

Library of Congress Cataloging-in-Publication Data

Ireland, Karin.
Albert Einstein / Karin Ireland.
p. cm.—(Pioneers in change)
Bibliography: p. 103
Includes index.
Summary: Traces the life and work of the physicist whose theory of relativity revolutionized scientific thinking.
1. Einstein, Albert, 1879-1955—Juvenile literature.
2. Physicists—Biography—Juvenile literature. [1. Einstein, Albert, 1879-1955.
2. Physicists.] I. Title. II. Series.
QC16.E5I74 1989
530'.092—dc20
[B]
[92]
89-6424
CIP
AC

CONTENTS

Albert: A Difficult Student

Albert Einstein was a man of opposites. He didn't talk until he was three, and for several years after that his parents and teachers thought he might be retarded. Yet as an adult, many people considered him to be the greatest scientist in the world. As a child he hated the strict discipline of the German schools. Yet he disciplined himself to ignore things that interested most of his classmates while he investigated the laws of physics instead.

He was a German who hated Germany and a man who wanted peace between nations. Yet he spoke out in favor of developing the atom bomb. He was rude and impatient with anyone who didn't have an open mind. Yet he could also be a very gentle and sensitive man and sometimes even a clown.

Albert Einstein was born on March 14, 1879, in Ulm, a small town in Germany. No one in his family had ever been especially gifted in science or math. Most of his relatives had been farmers, office clerks, or salespeople in small shops. His father, Hermann, owned a wine tavern and a small electrical and engineering workshop in town. The money used to buy these businesses had come from the family of Albert's mother, Pauline.

Hermann Einstein was a good person. He was helpful and friendly—maybe too helpful, too friendly. He had a hard time saying no when some of his customers asked for lower prices or for loans. Finally he lost so much money that he had to close his shop and look for another way of making a living.

Hermann's brother, Jakob, was an engineer. He offered to open a shop with Hermann making and selling electrical equipment if Hermann would move to Munich. Hermann agreed. In 1881, the family moved from Ulm, a small country town where it was common for cows to be herded down the main street, to the bustling city of Munich. There Jakob kept up with all the latest scientific developments, especially those that could affect the sale of the equipment he and Hermann made. The brothers worked hard, and the business was quite successful.

When Albert was two and a half years old his sister, Maja, was born. From the very first day he adored her. They became close friends, and he would do just about anything she wanted him to do.

Most children begin to say words when they are about one year old. Albert didn't talk at all until he was three. Later, when cousins or neighborhood boys asked him to play, he would simply turn and walk away. He wasn't interested in the silly games they played. He would sit for hours watching ants working around a hole in the ground. He would spend days patiently trying to make friends with

Albert at five years of age, with his three-year-old sister, Maja.

the chickens that ran loose in the overgrown backyard. And he was always interested in nature, always trying to figure out how things worked. As an adult, he remembered something that had happened when he was four or five years old.

He was sick in bed, and his father had shown him a pocket compass just to keep him busy. As Albert turned the compass around in his hand, he noticed that the iron needle always pointed in the same direction! The more he thought about it, the odder it seemed. Something—out there—was making the needle do that. But he'd been told that there wasn't anything "out there," that space was empty. His father had tried to explain that forces at the North Pole attracted the magnetic iron needle. But that just made Albert think of more questions, and his father had run out of answers.

When Albert was five, he started elementary school. In those days in Germany, elementary schools were private and were run by various religious groups. Although Albert's parents were Jewish, there were many rules of the religion they didn't follow. They saw nothing wrong with sending Albert to a Catholic school. The Einsteins were freethinkers. They did what they thought was reasonable rather than what was expected. The Catholic school was closer to home and cheaper, and it had a good reputation. Why pay more to send him to a school that was farther away, more expensive, and perhaps not as good? Perhaps his parents' impatience with following rules just because they *were* rules helps explain why Albert became such a difficult student in school.

Albert was a good-looking little boy. He had dark curly hair and big brown eyes. But he was obviously different from the other children in his school. For one thing, he was the only Jew in the entire school. For another, he still didn't talk very well. Even when his speech improved, he hesitated and took his time to think about the questions people asked him. His instructors called him "Herr Langweil," meaning "Mister Dullard." In other words, they called him stupid right to his face.

There were other things besides his slowness that made Albert's teachers angry. Whenever a lesson bored him, he got a dreamy look in his eyes. At these times he didn't even pretend to pay attention. Whenever a lesson *did* interest him, he always had too many questions! Instructors didn't want children to ask questions. They didn't want to have to explain what things meant. They wanted the students to memorize their lessons and "behave." Students who caused trouble were beaten or hit on the palm of the hand with a sturdy ruler.

Albert never complained to his parents. But he began to hate school. He hated the teachers who frustrated him so. Actually, his parents probably wouldn't have been able to help if he had complained. Albert's school was no more brutal than other schools of the time.

At home, though, he was free to do whatever he wanted to do. At home questions were answered when they could be, and he was loved. His parents were nice people. They made friends easily, and neighbors came to their house for quiet evenings of music and good conversation. Some evenings, as Pauline played classical music on the piano, Albert would tear himself away from his books to join her on his violin.

Albert grew up during a time of political unrest in Europe. During this period, the German army was growing larger and stronger. There was a possibility that the country would find itself at war with Russia in a struggle for power. Germany was also keeping a careful eye on France, another country that was working to make its army stronger. German soldiers were famous for their bravery and their obedience to orders. The nation was determined to maintain that reputation as a warning to neighboring countries. Officers paraded around in the streets, looking very powerful and stern. Albert's schoolmates were impressed with the uniforms and with the shiny brass as the bands marched by. They played games in which they pretended to be soldiers. But not Albert. He had books to read, things to study. Even at such a young age, he thought it was wrong for people, like the German soldiers, to rule other people by force.

In 1889, when Albert was ten, he entered the Luitpold Gymnasium, a secondary school. There children were taught the basics of Latin and Greek, history and geography, and simple mathematics. The method of instruction was the same as it had been at the Catholic school. Students were expected to memorize their lessons and not cause the teachers any trouble.

Albert was still slow to answer when people questioned him. And socially, he was backward. He said what he thought and didn't realize, or perhaps even care, that his words might hurt others' feelings.

Albert's uncle Jakob would sometimes teach him math. His uncle Cäsar, his mother's brother, helped awaken his interest in science. When Albert was twelve, he was given copies of A. Bernstein's *Popular Books of Physical Science* and L. Buchner's *Force and Matter*. He read the books carefully. Soon he became even more interested in mathematics. He enjoyed working out the problems in the books by himself. Most of the time he kept to himself. More and more he thought and wondered about how the universe worked. How did light travel? Why did electricity work? Were Newton's laws of gravity correct?

By the time he was 13, Albert was reading and understanding scientific material that many adults would have found impossible to follow. The more he learned, the more he began to doubt ideas that everyone else accepted as facts. He began to question some of the laws scientists had come up with to explain how the universe worked.

Albert also compared what he read in science books with what he was being taught about the Bible. He began to doubt some of the religious teachings taught at school. In fact, he began to think that the teachers and the government were lying to students on purpose. That feeling made him distrustful of anyone in authority. He didn't believe his teachers unless he could prove that what they said was true. He didn't even believe what scientists of the day thought. He refused to accept their solutions if those solutions didn't make sense to him.

Even as a boy Albert could work on one problem for months. He could hold the idea in his mind, examining it from one angle then from another. In class, when he wasn't solving a problem, he was asking questions. The instructors at the gymnasium didn't like his questions any more than the teachers at the Catholic school had. His classmates thought he was a show-off. They teased him for being a Jew. Anti-Semitism—being hostile to or discriminating against Jews—was illegal. But instructors didn't come to his rescue. Instead, they looked the other way.

The more Albert worked to learn from his own books, the less he cared about anything else. His classmates talked about their friends, the latest fashions, or their plans for the evening or weekend. Albert had no interest in any of these things.

All the while Albert was busy with his studies, the

Albert Einstein at age fourteen.

political situation in Germany continued to change. The army was becoming more and more powerful, and citizens were ordered to do business only with shops that were run by military people. As a result, many shopkeepers lost so much business that they had to close down. When an electrical shop run by military people opened down the street from Hermann and Jakob's business, people were afraid not to take their business to the new shop. The Einstein business failed, and Hermann found himself out of a job again.

Albert's mother had wealthy relatives in Italy. They wrote that there was a store in Milan that Hermann could buy. The small store sold things like hammers and saws, soap, flour, fabrics, and clothing. So once again, the family packed to move. Albert was excited when he heard about the move. He hated school. Even more, he hated knowing that within three years he might be called into the German army. It was a blow to hear that he would have to stay in Munich to earn his diploma. But he was too obedient to argue with his father about it.

Albert was 15 when he watched his family board the train that would take them across the Alps to Italy. Albert moved his things across town to the home he would share with distant relatives. He felt very much alone.

Albert's father wrote him letters from Italy in which he described the country and the people. Hermann made Italy sound like the most wonderful place in the world. This made it harder for Albert to stay in Germany. While life wasn't easy for him, he wasn't making it easy for his teachers either. One of them angrily told him to leave school. Albert was furious. He wanted to leave, but it was one thing to leave voluntarily and another to be thrown out. It just made him hate Germany and its horrible, self-righteous people even more. Albert stayed in school. But he came up with a plan that would make it possible for him to leave without having his records say he was expelled. He convinced a doctor to give him a medical leave. The doctor agreed to write that the stress of being separated from his family had made Albert ill.

It has been written that Albert renounced—that is, gave up—his German citizenship on the way to Italy. As much as he would have liked to, at the age of 15 he was probably too young to do anything legally. According to a letter now in the archives of the Princeton University library, he begged his father to help him end his German citizenship. His father doesn't seem to have done anything about it then, though. Still, Albert refused to consider himself a German. On forms where he had to fill in his nationality, he wrote, "son of German parents."

Albert liked Italy, with its rolling hills and green countryside. The sunshine was warm, and the people seemed friendly and free. He read, lazed in the sun, and questioned peasants about the way they lived. Albert kept up with his own studies, trying to figure out the puzzles of the universe. He would probably have been happy to stay there forever, but his father began having financial troubles again. Hermann's health was failing. He couldn't work the long hours it took to be successful. He had decided that Albert should become an electrical engineer. He urged his son to return to school and prepare for this career.

To Albert school was a prison he had finally managed to escape. The thought of returning made him unhappy. But he knew his father wouldn't be able to support him much longer. Reluctantly, he agreed to go back to school. His Italian wasn't good enough to allow him to study in Milan. He'd have to study someplace where subjects were taught in German. There was also the problem of a high-school diploma. Albert didn't have one, and he refused to go back to Germany to get it.

Fortunately, there was another possibility. German was one of the languages spoken in Switzerland. The Swiss Federal Polytechnic School in Zürich was one of the best technical schools in central Europe. It was the one university where students did not need a diploma to enroll. However, those who wanted to enter had to pass the entrance examination. Albert was 16, at least two years younger than most of the students who would be starting there. But he agreed to take the test.

Albert took the examination in Switzerland and scored

very high in mathematics. But he failed miserably in French, English, zoology, and botany. The Swiss Federal Polytechnic School refused to accept him as a student.

Later, as an adult, Albert admitted that it was entirely his fault that he failed the examination. Even though he had agreed to return to school, he just couldn't bear the idea of becoming an engineer. He didn't like work in which he would have to use inventive brain power to create things that made everyday life more complicated. He hadn't studied for the test at all.

Even though Albert wasn't admitted, the director of the school asked to talk with him. The director was impressed with Albert's mathematics scores. He seemed to feel there was something more to the boy than his other test scores indicated. He persuaded Albert to attend a preparatory school nearby. The director felt that Albert would be able to enter the polytechnic after a year at the school in Aarau.

Albert was pleasantly surprised with the school in Aarau. It wasn't like the schools in Germany. For one thing, students didn't have to take military training. For another, they weren't expected to learn by memorizing their lessons word for word. And sometimes students and professors even worked together. The best part was that Albert had convinced his father that he would be a terrible engineer and that he should study for a teacher's degree instead.

The more Albert learned about mathematics, the more he saw how specialized it was. There were too many different branches of mathematics, and too much to know in each one, for anyone to understand it all. He began to pay more attention to physics, the science that deals with matter, energy, motion, and force. He decided this would be a better way to seek out the answers he needed.

Albert went back to Italy to spend the Christmas holiday with his family. While he was there, Albert continued badgering his father to end his German citizenship for him. Hermann finally gave in and wrote to the authorities. On January 28, 1896, Albert's German nationality was formally ended. For the next five years he would be stateless.

While Albert was in school his family sent him money for food and clothing. He saved much of this money for something else. Albert wanted to become a Swiss citizen when he became 21. For that, he would have to pay a fee to register an application. He was determined to have the money by the time he was old enough.

Albert completed his studies in Aarau with top grades and was admitted to the polytechnic. In late 1896, Albert entered the polytechnic in Zürich. He would study there for the next four years. If he graduated, he could qualify for a teaching job. Albert had decided that he really wanted to be a teacher. And he would be a *good* one, not like the narrow-minded people who taught in the German schools. Teaching would have another advantage: He would be able to spend his spare time with his own studies.

Albert's classmates at the polytechnic were people who had left their homes in Russia, Hungary, Germany, Poland, and even France to get a good education. They believed science belonged to everyone, not just to one nation or another. Albert agreed completely.

Because Albert had lived in Germany and Italy, some of his schoolmates thought he was quite a man of the world. He was five feet nine inches tall, had curly black hair, and a narrow mustache. His casual manner made girls like him, and he liked them, too. But he never got too close to any of them. Thoughts about physics and work on his theories always came first.

Even before leaving Italy for Zürich, Albert had sent a letter to his uncle Cäsar saying that he planned to tackle one of the most controversial scientific subjects of the time: The relationship between electricity, magnetism, and ether, that airlike gas that scientists believed filled all space.

The letter was handwritten, five pages long, and it outlined what scientists already knew about the subject. It wasn't much. But Albert felt scientists could learn more if they studied certain things, which he listed, and if they experimented. It was an impressive paper for a boy of 16 to have written.

Later, during the years Albert studied at the polytechnic, new discoveries in physics were being made. Theories of physics were constantly being changed. Albert liked the school. However, he still demanded difficult answers from his instructors. His know-it-all manner made him unpopular with these teachers, just as it had in Germany.

Albert recognized that his instructors were teaching out-of-date theories and ideas about physics. He also felt that many of his classes were a waste of time. Often he did his own research instead of going to class.

While Albert studied on his own, a friend went to all the lectures and took notes to share with him. In this way, Albert could pass the tests. When he did attend class, he wasn't always very polite. His questions often made it obvious that he knew more than his instructors did.

Albert was also required to spend time in the laboratory. Unfortunately, even there he got into trouble. Once he tore up the instructions and tried to do an experiment his own way. The resulting explosion injured his hand and made a mess of the laboratory. The instructor wasn't pleased. Albert's teachers thought he was one of the awkward students who might or might not graduate but who definitely caused a lot of trouble.

Albert had a small group of friends who stuck by him, though. One was the friend who shared his class notes. Another was Albert's physics lab partner, Mileva Maric. Mileva wasn't like most young women of the late 1890s. She believed women should be educated, and she was serious about her studies. She enjoyed listening to Albert's ideas, even though she didn't always understand them.

By the end of their studies at the polytechnic, Albert and Mileva were in love. They planned to get married soon after graduation—as soon as they both had teaching jobs. Actually, they believed that only Mileva would have to look for a job. Albert expected to be hired at the polytechnic, since students earning teaching degrees usually were.

In 1900, at the age of 21, Albert graduated. Because he missed classes so often he graduated with an average of 82 percent. This wasn't a particularly high score.

Still, that might have been all right if his attitude during those four years had been better. His teachers remembered the classes he had missed and the lab experiments he had failed. They remembered his challenging remarks and manner. All of his instructors thought he was too original, too independent. None of them thought he'd be successful as a teacher or a physicist. Not one of them would write a letter recommending him for a teaching position. He was not offered a job at the polytechnic.

Einstein's First Great Discoveries

It had never occurred to Albert that he wouldn't be offered a teaching job at the polytechnic. When he wasn't, he had no idea what he would do instead.

The day he graduated, the allowance from his family stopped. He had to think of something. Albert wasn't good at dealing with details like these. He went back and forth trying to decide what to do. The obvious move, of course, was to apply to other schools, and he did.

While he waited for replies, Albert began to think that perhaps teaching wasn't the answer after all. He had spent so much time and effort studying to pass the final examinations that he had lost all interest in classroom physics. Still, he wanted the kind of job that would allow him to continue his own research. But what if his research never led to any answers? Perhaps it would be better for him to work as a shoemaker or a lighthouse keeper and do his thinking during his spare time.

Although Mileva wanted very much to be married, she agreed to wait until Albert found a regular job.

A few months after graduation, Albert did manage to get a temporary job helping the director of the Zürich Observatory with mathematical calculations. The work wasn't challenging, but he didn't care. It earned him a paycheck. Equally important to Albert, it made him eligible to apply for Swiss citizenship.

Albert continued to send out job applications and write to friends that he was looking for a permanent job. During his free time he worked on his own research. In 1900, he had an article published in *Annalen der Physik*, a German physics magazine. In this paper, "Phenomena of Capillarity," Albert explained that surface tension works to keep water flat in a container. That tension pushes water against the edges, where the water climbs a fraction of the way up the sides of the container.

Albert's discovery wasn't important only because it explained what water does in a container. The discovery also helped explain other things that people had observed. Capillarity helps answer questions about how plants get water from the ground to their leaves. It also explains why, when a glass tube or straw is placed in a liquid, the liquid in the tube or straw rises above the level of the liquid outside the tube or straw.

After several months, Albert's application for Swiss citizenship was processed and he was asked to appear before an examining board. Members of the board didn't want to grant citizenship to people who might cause trouble, so they asked Albert for his opinion on various political questions.

Albert's opinion was that politics was a waste of time. His answers showed that he knew and cared very little about world affairs. The board decided that he was too naive to be a threat to national security. They approved his application. On February 21, 1901, Albert finally became a Swiss citizen.

Albert knew that all Swiss citizens spent three months training in the Swiss army. Even though he had hated the German military and would probably have rebelled against becoming a German soldier, he was actually happy to sign up for military service in his new country.

He told friends that the Swiss were more humane than people in the other countries in which he had lived. Switzerland was an honorable nation, he said, one that was sensible and sane. Being a soldier here, he told them, would be a privilege. Unfortunately, Albert had flat feet and varicose veins. The military doctor rejected him.

Albert thought that once he became a citizen, his chances of getting a job would improve. His temporary job at the observatory was over and by March he was still unemployed. Not sure what else to do, he went back to Milan to stay with his parents.

From Italy he continued to write letters inquiring about work. He also wrote frustrated letters to Mileva. In some of those letters (made public in 1987), he wrote that his mother was furious about their plans to marry. Albert wrote that his mother ranted and raved that he was ruining his future and blocking his path through life. His mother warned that when he was thirty, Mileva, who was four years older than he, would be an old hag.

Albert didn't change his mind, though. He and Mileva met whenever they could. In 1901, she learned that she was pregnant.

According to Albert's letters, a baby girl was born. They named her Liese. From Italy Albert wrote Mileva that he was "dizzy with joy" and that he was trying to find a way to have the child stay with them. However, he wasn't successful. The letters don't say exactly what happened, but apparently Liese was raised by someone else near Mileva's childhood home.

Albert finally managed to find a substitute position in Switzerland teaching mathematics at a technical school. Two months later, however, the regular teacher returned. Next, Albert found a job tutoring a young English boy in a Swiss boarding school. But that job didn't last long either. He was fired because he wasn't strict enough to suit his employer.

Albert was living in Zürich again when he got a letter from his mother saying that his father was ill. Pauline also said she herself was not as strong as she had once been. Elsa, Albert's cousin, had gone to Milan to help them. Albert felt depressed that he hadn't made more of a success of his life. Here he was, a grown man, and there was nothing he could do to help his aging parents.

During this time one positive thing did happen. Albert completed a paper that was his thesis for his Ph.D. He sent it to the University of Zürich. Even though the paper wasn't especially important, he began to hope that he might bring some new answers to physics. But one question still haunted him—how would he earn a living?

Albert continued to write letters in search of permanent work. He sent one to a friend, Marcel Grossmann. Grossmann was the classmate who had shared his class notes with Albert at the polytechnic. Grossmann liked Albert and thought the school had treated him unfairly. He wanted to help if he could, so he took Albert's letter to his father. His father sent it to a friend of his, Friedrich Haller.

Haller was the director of the Swiss Patent Office in Bern. As a favor to Mr. Grossmann, Haller agreed to interview Albert for a job as a technical expert, second class. Albert's job would be to study new ideas for inventions that people described in a written application. Albert would compare these with products already in the catalog and determine whether or not each new idea would work. Inventors hoped to receive a patent, since once a patent was awarded, it meant no one could copy the inventor's idea.

Albert didn't have an engineering background, but Haller liked him. He offered Albert a position as technical expert, third class, one grade lower than they had originally discussed. The salary was less, but Albert accepted. He didn't really have much choice. It was the only permanent job he had been offered. He held this job from 1902 to 1909.

Actually, the job worked out well for Albert. He did the work he was supposed to do with the patent applications. But at the same time, a corner of his brain continued to work on his own questions. He scribbled notes on scraps of paper and shoved them into a drawer whenever someone passed by. When he left the office each day, he was free to concentrate on his own research.

Michelangelo Besso, an Italian engineer, sat at the desk near Albert. When work was slow, they talked about physics. Sometimes after work they went to a restaurant where others from the university met to talk.

Albert and Mileva began to make plans to be married. Friends had noticed a change in her, though. She was unhappy, and they were sure it was because of something Albert had done. When they asked, Mileva said it was a personal matter and refused to talk about it. Apparently she had never told them about Liese. But it must have made her

The house in which the Einsteins lived in Bern, Switzerland.

angry and sad to know that her baby daughter was being raised by someone else.

In January 1903, Albert and Mileva were married. Neither of them had enough money for a honeymoon. They celebrated with a dinner in a nice restaurant and then went to their new home, a small apartment in Bern.

Being married didn't make Mileva less gloomy. She had never wanted to spend her time cooking and cleaning. Yet that was just what she found herself doing. Albert included her in some of his projects, asking for help with mathematical work, but not enough. She wanted to do more; she wanted to be a partner. Unfortunately, she didn't understand his theories, and he didn't seem to want to explain them. He was silly and fun when he wanted to be, but he shut her out of his world completely when he was thinking.

Albert didn't want a partner in life as much as he wanted someone to take care of the home and make it a peaceful place for him. He didn't think that was unreasonable—it was what his mother had done. In fact, it was what most women did in those days.

A year later, Hans Albert was born. Mileva became a devoted mother. However, the situation between her and Albert didn't improve. It became worse. When guests came to the Einstein home, Albert played his violin and talked and laughed. But once the guests had gone, he retreated to his other world and his work on physics. Mileva was left behind.

Albert's imagination was always coming up with ideas for him to consider. He just seemed to know when one of those ideas was on the right track.

For years, he had been puzzled by questions of relativity. One area of interest concerned light. Scientists knew that all motion is relative to the person who is observing it.

For example, if Albert saw a train pass by going at 60 miles per hour, he knew that to people on the train it looked as if *he*, too, were going past at 60 miles per hour.

What about sound? If a whistle blew on that train, would the sound travel 60 miles per hour faster than usual in the direction in which the train was moving and 60 miles per hour slower in the opposite direction? The answer is yes. Albert, on the ground, would hear the whistle after people on the train heard it.

Albert had had the imagination to consider that light might be different. Everyone knew that when a person on a train struck a match the light would travel toward him or her at the usual speed of light, 186,000 miles per second. But only Albert believed light traveled away from the train at the same speed. Albert would manage to solve one part of the puzzle, but that would lead to another. There were times when he thought so hard about relativity that he wouldn't eat. He couldn't sleep. He would wander around in a daze. When people spoke to him, he didn't hear.]

He tried to rest by concentrating on other problems. It was at this time that Albert did solve one important question about light. Scientists thought light traveled in waves, but he showed that a beam of light also acted as a shower of particles. This 1905 paper itself would have been enough to make him famous. It paved the way for the theory of quantum mechanics (which helps explain the movement and relationship of particles that are very small).]

Some people say Albert decided to give up on relativity and, when he did, he relaxed and the answer came to him. That may or may not be true. But later in 1905, the answer did come.

More than 200 years earlier, Newton's laws of physics

had been developed. Newton's laws appeared to work very well for everyday problems such as how far a ball will go when thrown a certain direction with a certain amount of force. They seemed to explain how high such a ball will bounce and how long it will take a train going a certain speed to stop.

Albert believed Newton's laws would not be accurate when solving problems with elements that are very small, very large, or moving very fast. They would not explain how very small particles related to each other or how long it would take a rocket to reach a certain star.

It took Albert five weeks of intense work to get his findings, which he called the Special Theory of Relativity, down on paper. He had proved, at least to himself, that Newton's laws of relativity did not hold true when explaining the relationship of very large or very fast things to other things of any size or speed. Albert didn't call his theory special because it was fancy. Albert called his theory special because it applied only to a special, or limited, set of circumstances (those dealing with the very large or the very fast). When he finished, he was so exhausted that he collapsed in bed for two weeks.

Only someone with an incredible imagination could have thought of the Special Theory of Relativity. Only Albert Einstein could have proved it. By thinking, and using mathematics, he proved that the speed of light is *not* relative. It doesn't matter whether light is going with or against motion; it always travels at the same speed. That was the Special Theory of Relativity.

When the paper was printed, some scientists shouted and screamed that it was nonsense written by an ignorant patent clerk. Others completely ignored Albert's discovery.

3

Early Career Changes

During the same year Einstein wrote the Special Theory of Relativity, he published other papers that would later cause the world to call him a genius.

As mentioned in Chapter 2, Einstein wrote a paper on light and presented his theory of the photoelectric effect. Scientists knew that when a beam of light is shown on a metal surface some electrons from the surface "jump out." Electrons are very small particles of matter. For some reason, the number of electrons that jump out increases as you shine more blue light on the metal. But no matter how much red light you shine on the metal, no electrons jump out. It was a puzzle to which scientists did not yet have an answer. That fact alone made them look for an answer.

Einstein explained that the energy carried in a beam of light is separated into bits, called photons. The energy of each photon depends on the frequency of the light. Frequency is the number of light waves that pass a place per second. Blue light has a higher frequency than red, for example. Red light has so little energy per photon that a single photon isn't strong enough to make an electron jump out of the metal. So no matter how bright the red light is (bright light has more photons), each photon hits only one electron and since it is not strong enough, no electrons jump out. Today this information is used in solar cells to turn the sun's light into electricity for heating homes as well as for generating energy in space satellites.

In another paper written in 1905, Einstein showed that mass (the amount of matter in an object) can be converted into energy and energy can be converted into mass. They are closely related. For example, an atom of uranium, broken in two, equals less mass but much more energy, since part of the mass has been converted into the heat, light, and radiation that made the explosion. And the reverse is also true. This led to the most famous formula in physics: $E = mc^2$. In words, this means energy (E) equals mass (m) times the speed of light (c) times the speed of light (c).

Skeptics, or those who doubted that his theory was true, asked Einstein how he proposed to release all this hidden energy. He admitted that his theory might not be useful. In order to get and use that energy, scientists would have to find a way to shatter an atom whenever they chose to. That didn't seem likely. There seemed to be no way of testing the theory, and therefore no way of using the information. For years Einstein thought his formula was just the result of his relativity theory and that it had no real usefulness.

When scientists believe they already have an answer to a question about the universe, they don't accept a new answer easily. And they don't like to accept it without proof. Einstein was never interested in doing actual experiments to prove he was right—logic and his mathematics were proof enough for him. Some scientists were beginning to recognize that Einstein's papers were the work of a genius, but most continued to say they were nonsense. The truth was that some of Einstein's theories were so advanced that many scientists simply didn't understand them.

Finally, in 1908, when Einstein was 29 years old, the directors of the University of Bern offered him a night position as a lecturer. Einstein liked the idea of being back at a university again. He was told that if he did well he would be promoted to the position of assistant physics professor.

The custom was for a lecturer to be paid based on the number of students he taught. Fortunately, Albert hadn't given up his job at the patent office. Only a few students took his course. Others drifted in but didn't stay long. He wasn't a very good lecturer. He wasn't prepared—he made mistakes and had to correct himself. Actually, he wasn't even teaching anything. He was just talking about various subjects that interested him.

By the following year, Einstein's name and theories were being discussed by top scientists. He was offered a position as associate professor of theoretical physics at the University of Zürich. He accepted, quit the patent office, and moved his family back to Zürich. It was more expensive to live in Zürich. To make ends meet, Mileva took in students who paid for their room and meals. Einstein continued to think and to publish papers on his findings. He was invited to meetings to present his theories. Einstein's ideas were attacked by famous men, but that didn't bother him. He stood up to these men and answered their arguments.

In July 1910, his second son, Eduard, was born. When

Einstein wasn't teaching, he was often seen pushing a baby carriage up and down the streets. He liked his children, but his mind was often elsewhere. It is said that he would lay an open book on the blankets that covered the baby and become so interested in what he was reading that he would absent-mindedly push the carriage miles from home.

This concentration helped him unravel secrets of the universe, but it also nearly killed him. One day a friend from the university went to visit Einstein at home. No one answered the knock, but the door was unlocked. The friend walked in and discovered the professor slumped pale and lifeless on the couch. All the windows were closed, and the stove was hissing fumes. The friend threw open the windows and finally Einstein was revived. Einstein said calmly that he had been deep in thought and must have dozed off.

Einstein's classes at the university were filled, and his students loved him. He had learned to entertain his students. He used his hands to express himself and made jokes to hold their attention. There was something else that made him popular. Einstein remembered how frustrated he had been as a boy in school, so he made a point of stopping often to ask whether his students understood him. He was one of the few lecturers who actually invited students to interrupt him if they didn't understand.

Einstein didn't teach relativity in his classes. But he did discuss it with friends who met at a local restaurant to talk. Students showed up at the restaurant, too, and he became friendly with them. In those days it was rare for professors to be friends with their students. Einstein, however, had always ignored society's customs when he thought they were ridiculous.

Einstein soon found himself exchanging letters with

some of the most respected physicists in the world. Universities competed to get him to join their staff. The German University in Prague, Czechoslovakia, let it be known that they would be interested in having him. Einstein let it be known that he would accept a position in experimental physics there if they made the offer. It was true that he had never been good at experiments, and he was sure Mileva would complain about living there. But the university had a good reputation. In Prague he would be a full professor rather than an associate professor. His salary would be higher—nearly double.

There were complications, though. The university required every member of its staff to be a member of a recognized church. Einstein was known to be an "unbeliever." Another complication was that he would have to agree to become an Austro-Hungarian citizen.

Eventually the university worked around the religious problem. Einstein agreed to take Austro-Hungarian citizenship as long as he could keep his Swiss citizenship, too. Mileva wasn't happy about the move, but the Einsteins arrived in Prague in March 1911 anyway.

Prague was filled with grand palaces, royal parks, and lavishly decorated churches. It was also filled with beggars, disease, and fleas. With the extra money Einstein would earn in his new job, he could afford a large apartment and a live-in maid. The Einsteins had used kerosene lamps in Bern and gaslight in Zürich, but this flat had electricity!

At the university, students enjoyed the sessions with Einstein, partly because they were never sure of what would happen. Einstein had never been good at experiments, and they didn't always work. He gave lectures about Isaac Newton and his laws of gravity. Gradually he became convinced that Newton's laws weren't quite accurate. These laws worked well enough for everyday situations but on a larger scale—for instance, when stars in space were being discussed—the slight error would make a big difference.

Was light bent by gravity as it passed near the sun? Newton believed gravity was a force that affected only objects that have mass. Light does not have mass, so Newton believed it could not be bent. Einstein thought Newton was wrong. He thought energy and mass were closely related and in some ways different aspects of the same thing. He believed gravity was a field that should affect both energy and mass. Einstein thought that when light passed the sun, it was deflected, that is, its path was bent as it passed near the sun. Furthermore, he reasoned, the degree of deflection could be calculated. He believed that when we see a star whose light appears near the sun, the star is not really where we see it. What we actually see is the light of that star after it has been deflected by the sun. Einstein was sure he was right because it seemed so logical.

Einstein spent almost every spare moment trying to find a mathematical way of proving his theory. He wrote a paper describing it. He knew most of his readers wouldn't believe him. He therefore offered a way for experimental scientists to prove that what he said was true. He said that when the sun is hidden—for example, during a total eclipse—scientists would be able to measure the displacement of the light from these stars. All they had to do was wait for an eclipse of the sun and measure the placement of the stars before and during the eclipse.

While Einstein was up to his bushy hair in calculations, the political climate in Prague was growing more tense. He still wasn't interested in patriotism, nationalism, or racism.

He still believed people were people and that all people and nations should cooperate and share. But the hostility between the Czechs and the Germans, and of the Germans toward the Jews was hard to ignore. Einstein solved the problem for himself by declaring himself a Swiss Jew and ignoring his German background.

In November 1911, Einstein was invited to a physics congress in Brussels, Belgium. It was a meeting of the most important physicists. The invitation meant that he had been accepted by the top scientists in the world.

When Einstein returned from the conference, Prague seemed depressing. He wasn't well, and it turned out that he had an allergy to the local water. When he was offered a professorship at his old school, the polytechnic in Zürich, he accepted. In August 1912, the Einsteins moved back to Zürich. At the age of 33, Albert Einstein returned as a full professor to the school that had failed him on his first entrance examination and had later refused to give him even the lowest teaching job.

Einstein began to work harder on extending his ideas on relativity. The Special Theory of Relativity was something that could be applied only to observers moving at different constant speeds. But what happens when the speeds change? What happens when one observer speeds up or slows down with respect to the others? Does he or she see the experiment differently than the observer does? Questions like these buzzed around in his head constantly.

Once he was involved in a thought, Einstein found it hard to put it aside. One story tells of students seeing him standing under a lamp during a snowstorm. He handed his umbrella to his companion and jotted down formulas for ten minutes as the snowflakes fell on his notebook.

It became fashionable to invite Einstein to parties. But Mileva could tell which hosts just wanted to show her husband off, and she turned down their invitations.

Max Planck, a famous German physicist, had been following Einstein's work. He believed in relativity and recognized that Einstein was a genius. Germany was already known for having some of the top scientists in the world. The country's leader, Kaiser Wilhelm II, intended to make the nation home of the best in every field. Planck became determined to bring Einstein to Berlin, capital of the German Empire.

Toward the end of 1913, Planck went to Einstein with an offer. If Einstein would agree to move back to Germany, he would be appointed head of the Kaiser Wilhelm Physical Institute once it was organized. Not only that, but Albert would be made a member of the famous Royal Prussian Academy of Science. This was one of the oldest, most outstanding scientific institutions in the world. To top it off, he would be given a special professorship at the University of Berlin, where he could lecture as much or as little as he wished. The rest of the time he would be free to do his own research.

It was a fantastic offer, especially for a man who was just 35. Einstein was constantly worried about earning enough to support his family. If he went to Germany, his salary would be high and he would no longer have to worry about money. He was still trying to work out the mathematics that would prove that gravity was a field, that light was bent by gravitation. In Zürich he was having trouble finding enough time for his research. And there was no one there who understood his theories well enough to help him. If he took the position in Berlin, he would be able to devote nearly all his time to research. Since the city was the center of scientific research, there was actually a handful of people who really understood his work. There was no question about it: This research was the most important thing in his life.

But as tempting as the offer was, there were serious drawbacks. Mileva hated Germany. And Einstein remembered the way Germany had been when he left. Jews were persecuted. Every citizen was under the thumb of the military. Things might not have changed much since then. Germany was trying to convince the world that it was superior in all matters. Einstein knew he could never do his best work if he had to be involved in stupid debates about which nation or race was the best.

He thought he knew one way to guarantee that he would be left out of what he considered to be mindless competition. Switzerland was neutral. When there were national conflicts, it did not side with one country or another. Einstein told Planck he would accept the offer to return to Germany, but only under one condition. He would have to be allowed to go as a Swiss citizen.

Planck knew the kaiser wouldn't like hearing that news. How could Germany boast about a Swiss scientist? Einstein knew very well that the kaiser might refuse his terms. His future now lay in the German kaiser's hands.

CHAPTER

4

Einstein Returns to Germany

The kaiser wanted the world to see Germany as the nation with the greatest artists, the greatest musicians, and the greatest writers, philosophers, and scientists. He didn't like the idea of having a great German institution headed by a Jew who called himself Swiss, but he knew Einstein *was* the best.

Planck convinced the kaiser that people would forget about Einstein's Swiss citizenship once the man was back in the country in which he had been born. Soon everyone would think of him as German, and any work he did would be credited to Germany. Planck returned to Switzerland to make Einstein a formal offer.

Mileva wasn't happy when Einstein told her he was going to accept, but she wasn't surprised either. She knew her husband would go wherever he thought he could do his best work. Mileva still followed physics enough to know that he would work best in Berlin. In April 1914, the Einsteins packed up their belongings and headed for their new home.

Mileva hated Berlin the minute she saw it. People there were cold and formal, not friendly as they had been in Zürich. The city was plain. The military was everywhere. It frightened her to think that her sons would have to be soldiers in the German army when they grew up.

Hans Albert hated the strict discipline of the German schools as much as his father had. Eduard was too young for school. To him one place was as good as another as long as his mother was there.

It felt odd to Einstein to be there. Years earlier he had managed to escape from this country. From then on he had refused to be called a German. But coming back as a famous scientist did make a difference. Now he had an office at the academy. The Prussian State Library, one of the best in the world, was just a few steps away. He had lunch every day with top scientists, and he attended seminars where the latest discoveries in science were discussed. Einstein was able to spend nearly all his time on his work. This was a side of Germany he hadn't been part of before.

The Germans had a strict dress code, and Einstein's baggy pants and loose sweaters did not follow it. A German professor was supposed to attend many social functions. Einstein felt that most of them were a waste of time. Still, he decided that it would be smart to put up with some of the Germans' rules at least some of the time, even when he thought these rules were silly. Einstein had privileges no other scientist had. He realized it would not be wise to make the others jealous.

One of the first lectures Einstein gave in Berlin was about his theory that gravity bent light. The theory didn't

Einstein's first wife, Mileva, and their two sons, Eduard and Hans Albert. This photograph was taken in 1914, the year Mileva and the boys moved back to Switzerland and the year World War I began.

change the way people looked at the relationship between most things. However, it would matter if someone were calculating the distance of stars in space or the route to reach them. Though he worked on it constantly, he still hadn't been able to prove his theory mathematically. But he still believed he was right, that gravity *did bend light.* Others believed just as strongly that it didn't.

While Einstein was working and his theories were being argued, Mileva stayed home and took care of the children, as she had always done. She complained, but Einstein was too busy with his work to hear.

After a few months, Mileva had had enough. When Hans Albert got out of school for the summer, she and the boys returned to Switzerland for a vacation.

When Einstein had first written about his theory that light was influenced by gravitation, he said it could be proved during an eclipse of the sun. During an eclipse of the sun, the moon would move between the sun and the earth, completely blocking the sun's lights. Scientists could then take measurements of the stars in relation to the sun *before* and *during* the eclipse. If the measurements were different, Einstein's theory that the sun created a gravitational field around itself that deflected the light of the stars would be proven.

Four German scientists took him up on his challenge. There would be an eclipse in August 1914 that would be visible from Russia. The four raised money to buy expensive telescopes and cameras and made plans for their trip.

As the date for the trip drew nearer, Einstein found it hard to think about anything but the experiment. He was always doing last-minute calculations, even when he was with other people. There is one story that at dinner with friends he finished eating, pushed back the plates, and began marking the hostess's expensive tablecloth with equations as he talked with his host. Another story is that at times when there wasn't a table handy to write on, Einstein would kneel down on the floor and scribble diagrams and equations on a scrap of paper placed on a chair.

Meanwhile, many European nations were taking sides over the latest squabble—a territorial disagreement between Austria and Serbia. Germany sided with Austria, and Russia sided with Serbia. Einstein had never taken part in discussions about politics, but even he knew tempers were getting very hot. In June 1914, supporters of Serbia killed an important member of the Austrian nobility.

In July, Austria declared war on Serbia. Then Germany

ordered Russia to end its military support of Serbia or risk war. When there was no reply, Germany declared war on Russia. Two days later, reasoning that France would join Russia in the battle, Germany declared war on France, too.

On August 4, Germany invaded Belgium. England was outraged at the barbaric act and declared war on Germany. World War I had begun.

Einstein was horrified at Germany's attack and said so to his colleagues the next day at lunch. He had always hated people or nations who tried to rule others by force. He was sure his colleagues at the university felt the same way. But he was wrong. These men were Germans, and German patriotism, drummed into every citizen practically from birth, was stronger than reason. The Germans weren't the only patriotic citizens, though. Many scientists in countries fighting Germany rushed to their governments to offer help.

Einstein, the lover of peace, was sad to learn that so many men he had admired were now working to develop new kinds of guns, airplanes, and even poison gas. To him, using science for war was just about the worst thing anyone could do. After seeing his fellow workers' hostility to his remarks, Einstein reminded himself that there was nothing he could do. As a Swiss citizen he was neutral. He closed his mouth and went back to his studies.

Unfortunately, the German scientists who traveled to Russia to record the eclipse arrived there on the day war broke out. They were arrested and taken to jail. Some historians say the scientists were kept there until the end of the war. Others claim their equipment was kept and the men themselves were traded for other prisoners and returned to Berlin. Whatever the case, the men were safe, but the experiment was canceled.

At home, soldiers did a goose-step march up and down the main streets. Booms, sounding like fireworks, could be heard as big guns aimed at far-off targets. Innocent people were caught in the explosions. Soldiers were dying on both sides in the battle zones.

German scientists were ordered to work on developing weapons the army thought would make the nation stronger. One day a notice was circulated ordering German physicists not to refer to the work of English physicists when they wrote scientific papers. Every day there were more orders, new rules.

Other European nations continued to cry out against Germany's brutality. Meanwhile, the kaiser attempted to justify his country's role in the war. A document titled "Manifesto to the Civilized World" was passed around the academy and University of Berlin. Scientists, philosophers, writers, musicians, and artists were asked to sign it. The document said that Germany was fighting to defend civilization against barbarians. It asked the world community of scientists to support the struggle.

Einstein was dismayed to learn that 93 German scientists had signed the paper. All his old feelings of hatred toward Germans and their country flooded back. Finally, Einstein could no longer remain quiet. It was a tradition that science was international. People worked together and shared results. Einstein felt that was the way it should stay. He and another pacifist—someone who opposes war and violence as a way of settling disputes—drew up a very different kind of document, "Manifesto to Europeans." This pointed out the insanity of the war and the damage it was doing to science. It attacked blind patriotism and showed the real causes of the war. It called on intellectuals to join forces in demanding a just peace and to work to create a united Europe. One hundred people were asked to sign. Only three or four did. Those who refused to sign the paper criticized Einstein for supporting it.

Many Germans considered Einstein to be a traitor. They complained that he wasn't doing anything to help Germany win the war. In fact, they said, he was working *against* Germany. Actually, any other German would have been put in prison for what Einstein was doing. But Einstein was protected somewhat by his Swiss citizenship and also by the fact that his research work was reminding the world that Germany did have the best.

Still, Einstein must have realized what an uproar this document would cause. It took courage to defy the kaiser publicly. It made him angry to see the people cheering in the streets when a new military victory was announced. Privately he hoped the "other side" would win. When Einstein learned of the New Fatherland League, which was devoted to outlawing war, he made a dangerous move and joined.

Historians do not know whether or not Mileva wanted to return to Germany at the end of the summer. But because of the war, she couldn't. She enrolled the boys in a Swiss school. Travel in a country at war was nearly impossible. Because of his Swiss citizenship, however, Einstein managed a trip to visit his family the following year. He had a good time with his sons and was sad when they asked whether they would be going back to Germany with him. He said no, he wanted them to be educated in Switzerland. He didn't add that he was getting a lot more work done without his family to deal with. The truth was that Einstein loved his children and his wife, but he didn't want them to interfere with his work.

Before he returned to Germany, Einstein looked up the French writer and pacifist Romain Rolland. Rolland believed a few dedicated men could stir up feelings of brotherhood and goodwill that would change the world. Einstein wanted to believe it was true. He offered to help Rolland in any way he could.

Rolland accepted Einstein's offer of help and sent him a steady supply of pacifist pamphlets and books. Einstein managed to have them smuggled to fellow pacifists who had been put in German prisons for saying what they believed.

Late in 1916, Mileva wrote Einstein that her brother, a medical officer in the Austrian army, had been captured by the Russians. Newspapers told of millions who were killed in one battle or another. Germany said it wanted peace but didn't act as if it did. It now seemed clear that what Germany really wanted was to win and rule the world. The war went on.

Submarine warfare had been restricted since early 1916 because the United States threatened to counterattack if any more unarmed American ships were torpedoed. On January 31, 1917, Germany told the United States that unrestricted submarine attacks would begin again. Two months later, the United States declared war on Germany.

Each day Einstein worked with men whose opinion of the war was completely different from his. While he worked for peace, he saw scientists whom he respected working on projects that were designed to kill. Whether he realized it or not, the strain was making him ill. At times the pain in his stomach made him double up in agony. Doctors said he had either an ulcer or an inflammation of the gallbladder. They treated him as well as they could.

When it was clear that Mileva would not be returning to

Germany, Einstein moved into a small apartment around the corner from his late father's cousin, Rudolf. Rudolf's widowed daughter, Elsa, lived in her father's house with her two young daughters. Einstein and Elsa had known each other when they were children. He knew that Elsa had helped his mother while his father was ill, but beyond that, the two had little in common. Elsa was a typical *hausfrau*—that is, housewife, a woman who was happy to spend the day shopping and cooking and cleaning. She was devoted to her family.

Elsa was an excellent cook, too, and she managed to serve tasty meals even though food was scarce. Since Einstein was a neighbor, and a relative, Elsa invited him to eat with them. When he became too ill to take care of himself, she urged him to move into their house. He was so sick that he wasn't able to put up much of an argument. He spent weeks in bed, often in terrible pain. During the first two months of his illness, he lost 56 pounds. Friends thought he might die. At times he thought so, too. Elsa stayed at his bedside, making him take medicine and soup. He slowly began to recover.

By late 1917, Einstein was finally well again and was able to return to his work at the academy. He never did return to his own apartment, though. Tongues wagged, but he didn't bother to explain to gossipers that he had his own bedroom and even ate many of his meals alone.

Mileva heard about the arrangement and wrote him an angry letter. She had always felt that eventually she and Albert would be together again, but this did not look good. She demanded to know Albert's plans for the future. He hated having to think about these kinds of things. But he knew that his love for his work was too strong to allow him to leave Germany. He was nearing 40; perhaps he was slowing down. Despite the war and his anger toward the people, he was doing important work. He felt he still had a great deal left to accomplish, and he had to give himself every chance. Nowhere else would he have the time to spend on his research that he had in Berlin, and his work was his reason for being alive.

Einstein wrote to Mileva and told her that he would continue to support her and the children but that she should begin papers for a divorce. Once he was completely moved into Rudolf's flat, his books took over several shelves of the wall-to-ceiling bookcase—Shakespeare, Dostoyevski, Homer, Cervantes, two copies of the Bible, even a book called *The One Hundred Best Jewish Jokes.* Einstein loved to learn about everything. Einstein's room at Rudolf's house was the attic of the seven-story apartment house. He believed anything that wasn't necessary just got in the way, so there were no pictures on the wall, no carpet on the floor. A plain gray blanket covered his bed. He stopped wearing warm under-wear and pajamas, and later even stopped wearing socks. What good were socks? he asked. They only caused prob-lems by getting holes. Sometimes he stayed in his room for three days at a stretch, working and thinking. When he did that, Elsa left his meals at the door on a tray.

Despite his personal problems, Einstein had continued work on a new theory he was developing. He called it the General Theory of Relativity. Einstein had to use much more difficult mathematics than he had used in the past. In 1916, he had published a paper describing his new General Theory of Relativity. This theory described gravitation in a new way. It replaced Newton's theory of gravitation in explaining some natural events. Einstein explained how space, time, and mass were related to each other. He used his

*Albert Einstein in his study in Berlin, 1916, the year his General
Theory of Relativity was published. Two years earlier, he had become
a professor at the University of Berlin and the director of the Kaiser
Wilhelm Physical Institute.*

43

theory to predict how much light from a distant star would be bent when that light passed close to the sun. This prediction was different from the one he had developed earlier.

Meanwhile the war was still raging. Thousands of people on both sides died every day. There were shortages of food and not enough fuel to heat homes. Some of the Germans were against the war. But when they spoke out against their government, they were thrown into prison, or worse. Because he was famous, Einstein got away with more antiwar talk than did other German citizens. Still, he felt guilty that he wasn't able to do more for peace. To smother the feelings of guilt, he escaped into physics and during 1918 wrote more than a dozen new papers.

As Germany suffered one heavy military loss after another, citizens became frightened. They began to see that the military was *not* strong. The soldiers were dying, not winning. In early November 1918, the German military turned against their leaders and left the battlefields; people rioted in the streets of Munich. The kaiser was forced to give up his power. Germany had lost the war, and a new government took power. The leaders agreed to peace on the victors' terms.

Einstein relaxed, believing that militarism had been abolished in Germany and that people everywhere had learned a lesson and would work for peace. This seemed a good possibility. The terms of the peace treaty said that Germany would have to give up its military weapons so it would not be *able* to fight again. Einstein believed that the winning countries would give money to the new government to rebuild the country. Instead, the treaty demanded that Germany pay "reasonable amounts" of money to other countries for the damage it had done.

This was humiliating. If Germany paid what the treaty demanded, it would be many years before it could become prosperous enough to become a proud nation again. The country was filled with citizens who were hungry, unemployed, and ill. The future did not look promising. Germans were angry at having lost the war, and they resented the treaty.

Einstein shook his head, disappointed, and buried himself in his work. Through friends Einstein heard that London's Royal Society was curious about his theory that gravity bent light. On May 29, 1919, the next eclipse of the sun would be visible in two different parts of the world. The British planned to send teams to Sobral, a town in northern Brazil, and to Principe, a Portuguese colony on an island off the coast of West Africa, to see what they could learn. Somehow, even during the war, scientists had managed to raise money for sophisticated telescopes and photographic equipment. Now that the war was over, the teams could make the final arrangements for their expedition.

When Einstein's divorce from Mileva became final, Elsa suggested that they should be married. Elsa told Einstein that she herself didn't mind the neighborhood gossip about their living together. But she was afraid it would embarrass her daughters, Ilse and Margot.

Einstein and Elsa were cousins, but distant cousins. Besides, they certainly didn't plan to have children, so there was no reason they shouldn't marry. Elsa's friends thought he was odd. His hair flew every which way, he dressed in baggy pants and sweaters, and there was always a pipe hanging from his mouth. But Elsa didn't seem to mind. People at the academy gossiped and let it be known that they weren't very impressed with Elsa. She was five years older than Albert, overweight, and not especially attractive. She had very weak eyesight and didn't care what she wore. But she was a happy person, kind and gentle. Einstein didn't care at all what anyone else thought. In the summer of 1919, they stood together in a registry office in Berlin and Elsa became his wife.

Einstein returned to Switzerland to give the news to Mileva and his sons. Hans Albert, a husky boy of 15, was angry. Mileva barely spoke. It was not a happy meeting. All the same, Mileva was fair. She told the boys that Einstein was still their father and that even though he wasn't with them, he wanted their love and respect. Mileva agreed that he was a strange man in many ways but told the boys that their father was good and kind. She said he would be very hurt if they turned their backs on him.

In Berlin, Elsa and her daughters made Einstein a part of their family life. There was a food shortage, but Elsa was a wonderful cook and she made sure he ate well.

Elsa didn't understand anything about her husband's work, but she did know he was a genius and she enjoyed knowing he was special. She was happy to take care of him, to deal with all the details of running a house. She didn't have hurt feelings when he locked himself away with his research.

After the eclipse, the English astronomers took their photographs back to England so that they could be measured and calculated. These pictures would prove whether or not Einstein's theory about gravitation was correct.

Einstein could hardly think of anything else as he waited for the answer.

5

Fame and Controversy

When the astronomers looked at the photographs they had taken in Sobral and Principe, they knew Einstein's theory was correct. But no one wanted to make an announcement until they could study the photographs carefully and make measurements of the deflection.

Einstein was anxious to hear the result. It was one thing to know he was right and another to have it *proven*. He wrote to a friend in Holland asking whether he had heard any news. The friend wrote to another friend, who wrote back that the news was good.

On September 27, 1919, Einstein was officially notified in a telegram that began, "Eddington [one of the astronomers] found star displacement at rim of sun...." He went to Holland to learn the details from his friends. On October 25, at a meeting of the Dutch Royal Academy in Amsterdam, he heard the announcement that his General Theory of Relativity was correct. The press was not invited to the meeting. Except for the group of scientists there that night, few people were aware that a discovery had been made that would change their ideas of the physical world.

Finally, on November 6, the president of the Royal Astronomical Society of England made a public announcement that the photographic plates had confirmed Einstein's prediction. The rays of light *were* bent as they passed close to the sun. For the first time in 200 years, one of Isaac Newton's laws had been challenged and needed to be changed.

Normally this news would have made headlines in papers around the world, but the timing was bad. The following day, November 7, 1919, was the first anniversary of the end of World War I. It was this story that filled the front page in most parts of the world.

But Germany wasn't celebrating Armistice Day. It had lost the war and was still suffering. Passenger trains were being used by the government to carry coal and potatoes to towns where people were dying from hunger and the cold. Newborn babies died in cold hospital wards while parents and staff did their best to keep them alive. The people desperately needed something to boost their spirits, and Einstein's discovery was important news.

People who didn't know or care anything about physics loved him immediately. He dressed in odd clothing and was a common man, yet he was obviously quite bright. He was one of them, they told themselves, and he could see a future of prosperity and peace. The people wanted to believe he was right and turned toward him as their new hero.

Eventually the news of Einstein's discovery traveled to the rest of the world. Now everyone was talking about relativity, even though very few people knew what it was.

Newspapers and magazines printed page after page about the famous theory. Most of the time, though, they described the theory incorrectly.

Physicists all over the world lectured on the subject. Books were written to explain it, though many of them were inaccurate. Children were named after Albert. Cartoonists had a great time drawing him with his bushy hair and baggy pants to illustrate the latest jokes.

Elsa had a hard time dealing with all the people who showed up at their door to visit her husband. Hostesses wanted to show him off at parties, and scientists everywhere offered him research and teaching jobs in their countries. A representative of a tobacco company even came around to ask whether Einstein would agree to have his picture on a new line of cigars they wanted to produce. He said they planned to call them Relativity Cigars. Einstein was not happy to hear about that and did *not* give his consent.

Elsa began to screen the long lines of visitors who gathered at their door, turning away those she thought Einstein would not want to talk to. She also screened his letters, giving him only those she knew he would want to see. Many of the visitors and letters asked for autographs. Einstein had a hard time understanding why people treated him like a celebrity when all he had done was physics, but he gave his autograph to anyone who asked for it.

After a while he decided that if he had to sign autographs, at least it should do someone some good. From then on, he charged a small fee for each one and gave the money to a fund for starving war orphans in Vienna.

Everything Einstein said was immediately printed in newspapers around the world. Reporters asked him to describe his theory in 50 words or less, please. Others asked

Albert Einstein loved to play the violin. This photograph was taken in Berlin during the 1920s.

for details about his personal life. He considered these requests ridiculous and ignored them both.

With all the fuss, Einstein was constantly being interrupted from his work. Elsa knew how this bothered him. She found a house about 20 miles out of town where they could move and enjoy some peace and quiet.

During the war, Einstein had learned that famous people were listened to. He had taken advantage of his reputation and fame to try to promote peace and cooperation among nations. Now there was something else he had recently begun to support: Zionism, a movement that called for a homeland in Palestine for the Jewish people.

Einstein had always been too busy thinking about physics to pay attention to the discrimination he saw against Jews. But in Berlin it was impossible to ignore. Jews were being blamed for every problem the country had. Radicals insisted loudly that the only way to make Germany strong again was to get rid of the troublemakers. Many Jews were afraid and gave up their traditions hoping to blend in with other Germans and escape persecution.

What shocked Einstein most was that some Jews had become so ashamed of being Jewish that they became more anti-Semitic than the most extreme anti-Semites. These Jews refused to shop in stores owned by Jews; they turned their backs on Jewish friends. In discussions with others, they agreed that Jews were responsible for Germany's troubles. It was as though they felt they had to pay for something, even though they had done nothing wrong.

Although Einstein wasn't particularly close to most people as individuals, he loved and cared deeply about people as a whole. It pained him to see Jews suffering so. For generations, Zionists had been hoping to establish a nation in which Jews could be free to live in their traditional way. In 1917, the Balfour Declaration pledged British support for such a national home in Palestine, a part of the Middle East that Britain controlled. The more Einstein thought about the troubles the Jews were having, the more he felt that a homeland could make the difference between the survival or death of all Jewish people in his lifetime.

Germany seemed to have a new group in power every other month. Almost as soon as one group seized power, another group fought to throw it out. None was able to improve either the economic conditions of the country or the morale of the people. Other countries that had fought the war on their own land were not doing much better. Experts said 5 million people would die of cold and hunger during the winter of 1919–1920 unless countries began to work together.

Einstein had always encouraged countries to cooperate with one another. Now, since he was famous, people began to listen to him. Anti-Semites who wanted to rule the country didn't like that. They wanted people to listen to *them,* to believe that following *them* was the only way Germany could be strong again. They reminded confused people that during the war Einstein had stayed at the university working on his own projects. He had done nothing to help develop ammunition or bombs. They said that if he had worked on weapons instead of on theories, Germany might have won the war and there would be peace. And Germany would be strong instead of cold and hungry. To people who were cold and hungry, that sounded logical.

England and France were also struggling to recover from the war, and some of the people there resented hearing anyone who was German talk about peace.

53

Scientists in Europe had mixed feelings about Einstein. In December 1919 Sir Arthur Eddington wrote a letter telling him that he was being awarded England's Royal Astronomical Society's Gold Medal. Then, a few days later, Einstein got another letter from Eddington apologizing. The letter said that a group of hostile members had managed to gather enough votes against Einstein. That year no Gold Medal would be awarded. (In 1925, Einstein was awarded the Royal Society's Copley Medal and in 1926, the Royal Astronomical Society's Gold Medal.)

The general public also had mixed feelings about Einstein. On one hand, he received a standing ovation from more than 1,400 people who had packed a hall to hear him lecture on relativity. But a German anti-Einstein league was formed that offered a prize of money to anyone who could disprove Einstein's theories. One man even offered a reward for his murder.

In Paris, meanwhile, an American offered $5,000 through *Scientific American* magazine for the best 3,000-word article on relativity. Einstein told others he was the only one in his entire circle of friends who was not entering. He went on to say he didn't believe he could do it, and he wasn't joking. He believed the theory was simple to understand if one was a physicist and if one tried, but he didn't think he could explain it in so few words. Another man managed to do it well enough to satisfy the judges, though. It was quite a coincidence that the winner was a senior examiner in the British Patent Office.

Because of the threats that had been made on his life, Einstein's friends encouraged him to accept a position offered by the university in Holland. He could work and be safe. Einstein found the idea tempting. But he decided that if he left Berlin now, people might think he had been frightened away. He couldn't let anyone think that. He had to show that he had faith in the future of Germany.

"Berlin is the place to which I am bound by the closest human and scientific ties," he said. He stayed. He told friends that he had an idea he thought might help his struggle for world peace. If the Germans wouldn't listen to him because he had become a Swiss citizen, he would fix that. In order to show support for the German republic, he decided to take up German citizenship again.

He accepted offers to travel and give lectures. Despite the fact that he usually traveled with only one rumpled change of clothes, his lectures in Norway, Holland, and Vienna were always filled.

Einstein had learned a lot since his early days of lecturing students in a nearly empty hall. Now he talked in simple words and chose examples to explain relativity that everyone could follow. After his talks crowds cheered and called for more. Einstein would make a joke about not having worked out an encore to relativity and would play his violin instead.

One evening, after a lecture in Prague, a young man insisted on talking to Einstein. The man explained that he had considered Einstein's mass-energy equation and had concluded that it would be possible to use the energy locked inside the atom to make a powerful explosive. In fact, he said, he had invented a machine that could turn that locked energy into a bomb!

Whether the young man's equation was correct or not, his idea was. Twenty years later such a bomb—the atom bomb—killed more than 120,000 people and stunned the world.

6

The Nobel Prize Winner, the Jews, and the Germans

When Einstein returned to Berlin in 1921, the Zionists asked him to tour the United States to help raise money for the Palestine Foundation Fund. The Zionists needed money to help bring other Jews to Palestine and to continue building Hebrew University, which they had begun in Jerusalem.

Einstein was sympathetic, but he didn't like asking people for money and he said no. The Zionists would not let him off that easily. They reminded him that in dozens of countries Jewish students were being turned away from universities just because they were Jews. They told him that once the university in Jerusalem was finished, it could begin to educate some of these people. Einstein was all for education. The arguments convinced him, and he finally agreed to go along with Chaim Weizmann, a famous Jewish chemist living in England.

*Dr. Chaim Weizmann and Albert Einstein in the 1920s. Weizmann
was a noted chemist and Zionist leader who over a quarter of a
century later became the first president of Israel.*

Albert Einstein and his wife, Elsa, in 1921, the year he was awarded the Nobel Prize in physics. He actually received the award in 1922.

On April 2, 1921, Albert and Elsa and the Weizmanns sailed into New York Harbor. The difference between New York and Berlin was like the difference between day and night. Americans had not had to fight the war on their own land, and they were not suffering as people in Europe were. Buildings were all still standing, trains were filled with laughing people on holiday—not with lifesaving potatoes and coal. The people had jobs and homes to go to. They had fuel to keep those homes warm, and they had food to eat.

Even though his country had been their enemy, Americans had read about this peace-loving genius, and were willing to forgive. In America, Einstein was already a hit. When people didn't know the answer to a question, they would say, "Who do you think I am, Einstein?" Or, when something puzzled them they would say, "It's all Einstein to me."

All of New York knew the great man was on this ship. Einstein had no idea anyone cared! When a huge crowd swarmed the decks, he wondered what was happening. By the time he realize they had come to see him, it was too late to run. Flashbulbs popped, and reporters shouted at him to explain relativity in a few sentences.

Although Einstein didn't like reporters and was uneasy when they asked him questions, he could charm them when he wanted to. And he certainly wanted to charm them that day. The Jewish homeland needed money, and there was money in the United States.

When they went ashore the next morning, the Einsteins and the Weizmanns were guests of the city. Crowds waved Zionist flags and cheered as their long black car was driven down Second Avenue. Although he was hounded constantly, Einstein began to realize that Americans didn't mean to be rude; they were just enthusiastic.

Many who attended his fund-raising lectures didn't understand German, but they didn't mind. They were just eager to see him. As he talked, he completely won them over. After the first few towns on the campaign route, Einstein shortened his own talk and asked that the audience listen to Weizmann and acknowledge him as their leader. It made sense. Weizmann was a wonderful, passionate speaker—and he wasn't shy about asking for money.

The trip across the United States was long and tiring. For three months they arrived in towns by the morning train, waved to crowds as they were driven through the streets, ate breakfast at City Hall while listening to welcoming speeches, faced reporters at press conferences, ate lunch while enduring more speeches, attended meetings with important local Jews, then returned to a large evening meeting at City Hall.

When the meeting was over, they went back to the train and collapsed. By the next morning the train would have taken them to the next town, and the whole routine would start all over again.

Einstein had the authority to collect checks for Hebrew University, but many of the donors were reluctant to give theirs to him. They didn't think he looked very businesslike. Their instincts were probably right. Einstein had once used a check from a publishing house as a bookmark and forgotten all about it. It would have been lost forever if Elsa hadn't found it.

Einstein and Weizmann touched the hearts of American Jews. Money for the Palestine Foundation Fund poured in. By the end of the year, more than two million dollars had been raised.

While Einstein was on tour, people in Europe wrote and persuaded him to stop in England on his way back to Germany. He knew it wasn't the safest thing to do. Most English people still hated anything or anyone who was German, and that included him. But he decided that if he could help world peace, if even a few listeners would think more kindly of Germany as the result, it would be worth the risk.

The night Einstein was scheduled to appear in England, the lecture hall was filled. Security men from Scotland Yard watched the crowd carefully for any sign of trouble. When Einstein was introduced, the crowd just sat there, silent. As he spoke, in German, there was silence. When he finished and returned to his chair, there was still not a sound.

Then something odd happened: Someone started clapping. Then someone else, and someone else. Suddenly everyone was applauding, standing and applauding with their hands held high in the air. The cheering lasted for three long minutes as the crowd saluted him for his courage. One reporter wrote in his article for the *Nation:* "This is the turning point...sanity, understanding and harmony are being restored by men of creative genius...."

Back home in Berlin, Einstein turned all his energy toward his own research again. For months he worked in his attic on a unified field theory, trying to find the mathematical connection between electromagnetism and gravitation. If he could, it would be the first step in discovering the laws governing the conduct of everything in the universe. Perhaps there was no difference between gravity and electromagnetism—only different ways of looking at the same thing. He went for days without touching his violin. He was too busy thinking to sleep or eat unless Elsa reminded him.

In the spring of 1922 Walther Rathenau, a friend who was the German foreign minister, tried to persuade Einstein to take a break. Everyone knew there were still bad feelings between the Germans and the French. Rathenau told Einstein that his talk in England had helped mend the break between German and English scientists. He asked Einstein to try to do the same in France.

Einstein was tempted, but he said no. He told Rathenau he would do anything that would help, but he felt the hatred of the French toward anything German was so strong that they wouldn't listen to him. Rathenau said there was certainly no other way to win over the French. He begged Einstein to reconsider. Finally he agreed to make the trip.

Before Einstein left Berlin there were rumors that there could be trouble. He treated those threats the same way he treated the others: He ignored them. But he did agree to have his French hosts meet him midway on the train ride. As the train pulled into the station in Paris, they could see reporters and photographers crowded on the platform. It was late—midnight. There was nothing Einstein could say now that couldn't wait until morning. It would be safer to meet in the morning when security guards could control the crowd. He was like a schoolboy escaping the watchful eye of his teachers as he and his hosts sneaked off the far side of the train away from the crowd and ducked into a side door on another platform.

Just about everyone in Paris knew he was there to talk, but the audience was limited to scientists and students who had a special interest in physics. Security was tight, and invitations were carefully checked at the door. People had always had mixed feelings about Einstein, and things were no different in France. A few newspaper stories said he wasn't welcome there. Others said he was. One, taking a logical approach, reminded readers that Einstein was a scientist who had made great discoveries. French scientists could learn from his work. If a German were to discover a remedy for a disease, the paper asked its readers, would the French wait until peaceful relations were reestablished between the two nations before using that cure?

Before he left France, Einstein asked to be driven around the countryside where battles had been fought. He knew the war had been terrible, but he was still stunned to see how entire villages had been flattened and forests turned into scorched stumps by artillery fire.

At one large military cemetery where they stopped, Einstein saw endless rows of wooden crosses marking the graves of men who had died in battle. There were white crosses for the French and black ones for the Germans. He was close to tears as he told his friends, "All the students of

Germany must be brought here, all the students of the world, so that they can see how ugly war really is."

Two months later, a large group of French and German pacifists met for a friendship rally. They pointed to Einstein as proof that scholars can work together as brothers. The crowd cheered wildly.

Less than a month after that, Rathenau, the German foreign minister, was murdered by members of a German right-wing group. This group didn't want peace. It wanted power. It wanted to take control of the government, and its members believed that anyone who came between them and this goal had to be gotten rid of. A few weeks later, Einstein heard that he, too, was a target for assassination.

Friends made him stay away from the university, thinking the terrorists couldn't kill him if they couldn't find him. Elsa managed to keep him at home for two weeks. Then he rebelled. He learned that a pacifist group was planning a motorcade in which they would wave banners that said "No more war." Einstein went to the head of the line and sat in the back of an open car. He knew he was taking a big risk. But he could be very stubborn when he chose to be.

Einstein made it safely through the parade crowd, but friends insisted that he had to get away for a while. He had to leave Berlin. Because of Rathenau's death, he realized that they were probably right. It was late 1922, and relativity was known all over the world. Dozens of countries assured him that he would be a welcome visitor. In October, he and Elsa boarded a Japanese steamer for a six-month tour of East Asia.

When his ship pulled into Shanghai, Einstein found a five-day-old cable waiting for him. It said that the Swedish Academy of Science had awarded him the Nobel Prize in physics for his photoelectric law and for his work in the field of theoretical physics.

To some it seemed odd that the academy had chosen that particular theory to honor him for—it was 17 years old! His General Theory of Relativity was what had shaken the world! But when Alfred Nobel wrote the guidelines for awarding the physics prize, he said it should be for a "discovery," and that it should be a discovery from which humankind had gotten great use. Relativity was being used in laboratories. But no one could say humankind was affected in the way Nobel had meant. From the committee's point of view, though, Einstein was the most famous physicist in 200 years, and the academy couldn't ignore him forever.

When the news made the newspapers, both Germany and Switzerland tried to claim Einstein as their own. It was customary to award the Nobel Prize in Stockholm, Sweden, on December 11, the anniversary of Nobel's death. It was also customary for the ambassador of each winner's country to appear with the winner at the ceremony and at the state banquet given by the king of Sweden in his or her honor. Which ambassador—Swiss or German—would go with Einstein?

Switzerland pointed out that Einstein was traveling on a Swiss passport. Germany pointed out that Einstein had reclaimed his German citizenship, and that even if he hadn't, as a German civil servant he had automatically become a citizen in 1914 when he took the post at the university.

Einstein was still in East Asia as the prizes were being given out in Stockholm. As it turned out, this worked out well for everyone. He had a good excuse for not appearing at the formal event. The German ambassador went to

Sweden to receive the award on his behalf, and the Swiss ambassador presented it to him in Berlin.

On his way back to Germany, Einstein was invited to visit Palestine to see the work that was being done in the Jewish homeland. He saw the new hospitals, schools, and banks that had been built. He was moved at the sight of people working in the hot sun to build roads, and plant crops, to create a country out of bare, dry land.

Germany was still struggling to survive. Because the country was nearly bankrupt, Einstein's salary from the academy was next to nothing. He had been supporting both of his families with the extra work he did as a consultant to three large industrial companies. Now invitations to lecture were coming in from around the world, and these lectures added to his bank account. He decided to send the entire Nobel Prize check of $45,000 to Mileva although half of this money was apparently lost in the exchange from one currency to the other.

Mileva wrote that she was very grateful for it. She said that Hans Albert was doing well in school studying engineering and Eduard, or Teddy as he was now called, was 14 and brilliant. Teddy had his father's drive to learn about things, but he also had an incredible memory. He could remember everything he had ever read or heard. Einstein read the news and was proud of his sons. He was also happy that they were living with their mother.

By the summer of 1924, Germany was *still* a depressed nation struggling to survive. The value of the German money (called the mark) had gone down so much that one American dollar was worth more than four trillion marks. Germany printed so much of this almost worthless paper money that workers needed wheelbarrows to cart home their pay. Unemployment was still high. Salaries paid in almost worthless money could buy very little. There were still shortages of food and fuel. What small amounts of wealth Germany was able to produce went toward paying the debt for war damages it had caused to the other countries. Finally, the Allies took a softer view of the country and voted to reduce the amount of Germany's debt. They also agreed to make loans to Germany so it could rebuild.

This was a kind gesture. But it may have come too late. A young man named Adolf Hitler was busy stirring up hatred in Germans who were hungry enough and angry enough at the situation to listen. His message was not new. He said that the Germans were strong, a *superior* race. He said Germany's troubles had been caused by foreigners and Jews. Hitler reminded the masses that the war had been over for six years, yet Germany was still a defeated nation. He said that if Germany wanted to become strong again, it would have to get rid of the foreigners and the Jews.

Einstein was a highly visible target. He was a Jew, and he wrote papers and gave lectures warning against Germany's becoming a militant nation again. The more he spoke out, the more friends tried to convince him to leave Berlin for good. He told them he appreciated their concern but he just couldn't leave. At least not yet. Berlin had the intellectual climate in which he could do his best work.

Einstein felt that his time in Berlin was limited, so he pushed himself to work even harder than usual. Even when Elsa forced him to leave his office, he continued to do physics in his head. The lecture trips he made added to his stress. While on a speaking tour in Switzerland in 1928, Einstein collapsed. Doctors said he had an acute enlargement of the heart and would have to stay in bed for at least three months.

Elsa went to Switzerland to bring her husband back to Berlin to recuperate. "Recuperating" meant that for months Einstein wasn't allowed to smoke his pipe; nor was he allowed to have pencils or paper. Doctors wanted him to *rest*. To Einstein this was like being in prison. He accepted the situation a little better after Elsa hired a young German woman, Helen Dukas, to be his secretary. Helen helped them both. She supported Elsa when Einstein was feeling stubborn and didn't want to obey the doctors' orders. She also helped him by taking care of his mail and other simple paperwork.

Students were allowed to visit as long as they didn't upset him. His son Hans Albert, now a married man and an engineer with a Germany company, also came to visit.

By January 1929, Einstein thought he could see the connection between the laws of gravitation and electromagnetism. He believed they were actually different ways of looking at the same thing. He realized there was no way to prove that his unified field theory was correct. Yet he decided to write it up and send it to the printer anyway.

History seemed to be repeating itself. When they read the paper, some physicists clucked and said Einstein had had too much publicity. Others were reminded of what a genius he was. Some people even camped out on his doorstep hoping to get a picture, a glimpse even, of the man.

In March, Germany planned a celebration in honor of the fiftieth birthday of its celebrated son. A group of Zionists in the United States collected money to plant a grove of trees in Palestine to be named after him. A small observatory built

*Einstein enjoyed sailing in his sailboat, which was presented to him by
an important German bank in 1929.*

on a hill in Berlin was named after him. A bust of him was placed on the hill and unveiled as part of an impressive ceremony. Telegrams of congratulations poured in from around the world. Newspapers printed hundreds of stories about him.

Well-wishers dropped by to wish Einstein a happy birthday in person, but they found the house empty. He and Elsa had moved into the gardener's cottage of a wealthy friend to hide out until the craziness was over.

For their own celebration, Albert and Elsa built a vacation cottage in Caputh. Elsa carefully furnished a room on the ground floor to be his study. She had a desk placed in front of a window so that whenever he raised his eyes there was a view of the trees. She had bookcases brought in to hold his hundreds of books. Einstein loved the cottage. He loved the lake nearby, where he could sail. Still, as he looked around, he often felt guilty. He couldn't help thinking of how much good the money would have done for one of his favorite charities.

Later in the year, Einstein was again asked to give a peace lecture abroad. He agreed. He was sure that although Europe appeared calm, most countries were secretly building up huge collections of weapons.

All through October 1929, a group of Arab extremists killed Jews in Palestine. Einstein wrote a plea for justice to European and American newspapers. Didn't the world realize that the Jews had been given that land? Didn't they know the Jews had been working for ten years to build a nation in which they could live peacefully? Where was world support for their cause?

In Germany, Hitler's Nazi party was gaining support

and nationalism was growing stronger. Was the world going crazy?

In 1930, Einstein received several disturbing letters from his son Eduard. Eduard wrote that he hated his father, that he had been abandoned and doomed to a life in his father's shadow. This news was quite a blow to Einstein. He knew that Eduard had always felt he had to live up to his father's reputation, but he himself had done nothing to encourage this feeling. Einstein wasn't even sure why he *had* such a reputation. He was simply a man who worked very hard. Eduard wrote that he had struggled to win his father's love but felt that he never had. Now, at the age of 21, Eduard felt unable to go on.

Einstein went to Zürich to talk to the young man. He had always distrusted psychology, but after talking to Eduard in person, he knew that his son needed help. He paid for his son to go to the best doctors in the country.

Einstein returned to Caputh, but he couldn't forget the emotional pain his son was experiencing. He couldn't enjoy his country home, his sailing, or even his work. He was constantly thinking about Eduard. Friends watched the lines on his face deepen and his hair grow whiter. He stopped laughing. The light went out of his eyes.

In October's national election, Hitler's Nazi party went from 12 seats to 107 seats in Germany's lawmaking body. This was discouraging. At one point it seemed that Germany had begun to recover. Now it was beginning to slip, thanks to nationalism. Banks were failing, and the lines where the poor gathered for free soup were growing longer and longer.

Einstein felt powerless to help. In fact, friends pointed out to him that he might actually be unknowingly helping his enemies. Einstein was a symbol of Zionism, and because he was in the news regularly for one thing or another, people were reminded almost daily of Hitler's remarks. Einstein again considered renouncing his German citizenship and actually wrote a letter asking whether this could be done. But the letter was never mailed.

Einstein wondered whether his friends were right. Would it be better for everyone if he stayed out of sight for a while? He had been invited several times to visit the California Institute of Technology (Caltech) in Pasadena. When he was again invited to spend the winter there, he decided to accept. He, Elsa, and his new secretary, Helen Dukas, packed for the long boat trip.

Einstein was uncomfortable on the day they were to leave. As he closed the door to his cottage, he took a long, careful look at this home. He had a feeling they would never see it again.

7

The Man of Peace and the Atomic Bomb

Einstein liked California, and the people there liked him. Hollywood producers and actors threw a huge party in his honor. One producer even asked whether he wanted to be in a movie. While it was true that he had learned to add a little drama to his lectures, Einstein wasn't tempted.

During his two-month appointment to work and lecture at Caltech, he and Elsa lived on a quiet street near the campus. Many stories are still told about Einstein during this time. One tells of a friendship he had with a little girl. According to the story, she went to the house every afternoon. The two would sit on the Einstein porch trading news and eating cookies while he did her math homework.

When it was time for him to leave Caltech in March 1931, Einstein gave a lecture to the students on what he considered to be the improper use of applied science. In war, he said, applied science made it easy to kill people with more

Albert and Elsa Einstein arriving in California in 1931.

and more powerful poisons and bombs. In peace, it produced machines that made people's lives hurried and unrewarding. He urged the students to use their science for study and for peace.

While Einstein was in Pasadena, matters had grown even worse in Berlin. Hitler seemed to hypnotize crowds with his speeches. In order for Germany to be strong, he told them, it had to get rid of pacifists, foreigners, and Jews. He gained more followers every day. These people had no home, no job, and no hope. Hitler promised them that if they followed him they could together build a new and powerful Fatherland. People remembered the days when Germany *had* been strong. Germans had been proud. Many desperately wanted to believe Germany could be great again. They voted for candidates of Hitler's Nazi party. Others voted for Nazi candidates because Nazi storm troopers stood outside voting centers to make sure they did.

Einstein had been wrong when he closed the door at Caputh. After his term at Caltech was finished, he did return to his home. In Berlin he began speaking out again for the preservation of the old German republic, for cooperation between nations, for peace. He joined an organization called War Resisters International and urged the members to fight for peace. He pleaded with everyone to refuse to help in any preparation for war.

Einstein's search to find a way to prove that his unified field theory was correct continued.

Before the Einsteins left Pasadena in 1931, Einstein was invited to return to Caltech. In early December, the Einsteins again boarded a ship for the United States.

Einstein always seemed to be surprised by California. This time he couldn't understand how the people could be so unconcerned with the problems of Europe. Couldn't Americans see that by insisting that Germany pay its war debt they were forcing the country to remain in poverty? Didn't they understand that poverty was driving Germany to war again? He answered his own question: Americans, he concluded, didn't see anything. All nations thought only of themselves.

In 1932, representatives from 60 nations gathered in Geneva, Switzerland, to talk about peace. Their goal was to establish international laws that would prevent nations from attacking each other. Einstein went there to beg them to be flexible and not just think of their own countries. They listened. But no one was really willing to cooperate as much as they needed to, and the talks broke up after a few weeks.

In 1932, Einstein was again invited to return to the United States, this time to the proposed new Institute for Advanced Study in Princeton, New Jersey. Once it was opened, the institute would be open to men and women who had earned university degrees. There they could think and study without ever having to worry about classwork or grades, or whether the work they were doing was important to anyone but themselves.

If Einstein would agree to accept a permanent position there, he was told that he could spend all his time on his own research and give a lecture on his results once a year. In addition, he could name his own salary.

It sounded like the perfect offer, and Einstein wanted to accept. But he couldn't bear the thought of leaving Germany for good. He knew that in Berlin Nazi students were demanding that Jewish students be banned from the university. He knew that at least one Jewish student was beaten every day. He knew that Jewish professors were ignored or fired for no reason. He knew that a madness had taken over the country. However, he believed each day that the madness would have to stop soon. He believed that if he stayed in Berlin, he could help *make* it stop.

While most Jews tried not to call attention to themselves, Einstein continued to stand up and plead with citizens to ignore Hitler. Again, friends tired to convince him that he wasn't safe. They said it was only a matter of time before some hired thug came to kill him. Elsa heard the warnings and was so frightened for him that she walked around the house for days in tears. Finally, after months of thinking he would do one thing and then deciding to do another, Einstein decided what he would do once and for all. For five years he would spend five months of the year in Princeton and the rest of the time in Berlin. He would visit Pasadena once more, return to Berlin, then go to Princeton in October of the following year.

On January 30, 1933, while Einstein was in Pasadena for the third time in three years, Adolf Hitler was named chancellor of Germany. Einstein felt defeated. He had reasoned with people, pleaded with them to work for peace. Instead of listening to him, they had elected to power a man who believed that only the "true Germans"—those with blond hair and blue eyes, those who were tall and strong—should survive, reproduce, rule the world.

Einstein's appointment at Caltech was finished, and he didn't know where to go. Elsa said she didn't mind where they went, as long as they were together. Einstein couldn't stand the thought of never seeing his home again, of never sailing on the lake, never working with his colleagues in Berlin. But he knew this time he couldn't return. When a news reporter came to the apartment for a cheery farewell interview, she was given a world scoop.

"I'm not going home," Einstein told her. He told her that Germany was a sick country—a country that loved power and hated anyone who was different. He couldn't live there under those conditions.

News that began to come out of Germany proved that Einstein had been right when he warned people about Hitler and the Nazi party. Jewish physicians were fired from hospitals, and Jewish judges were thrown off the benches. People in Berlin were told not to shop in stores owned by Jews. People who spoke out against the government were murdered or sent off to concentration camps. Freedom of speech vanished. Books that didn't agree with Nazi thinking were thrown into piles and burned in the streets. It was a long time before Einstein could smile again.

In March, Einstein read in the newspaper that German Nazi storm troopers had ransacked his house. When they didn't find anything of interest, they took his sailboat. They also took the money in his bank account so he couldn't use it "for treasonable purposes."

Both Einstein and Elsa gave up their German citizenship and moved into a small house on the coast of Belgium. Helen Dukas, his secretary, joined them there. Now when he spoke out for peace, authorities in Germany accused him of being a traitor. Now that it was too late, other countries realized Einstein had been right. They couldn't do anything about Hitler, but they showed Einstein their support by offering him professorships at their universities.

In Germany, factories were working day and night to make ammunition, guns, and tanks. Einstein shared his fears with Sir Winston Churchill of England. He suggested that Britain and the rest of Europe should refuse to trade with Germany until it stopped preparing for war. But no one believed Hitler would be foolish enough to go to war. What in the world would he have to gain? He had all of Germany under his thumb. What more could he want?

But Einstein was so sure he was right that he made a decision to do something he would have found hard to imagine doing earlier. He actually spoke out in support of Europe building up a powerful defense. He recommended turning factories into makers of guns and ammunition. For the first time in his life, he said that European young men should be proud to enter the military service of their country.

Of course this new opinion made Einstein's pacifist friends think he was a traitor, and they said so loudly. They accused him of being hysterical about Nazi Germany.

Meanwhile, someone got word to Einstein that the Nazis had offered a reward of $5,000 to anyone who would kill him. Einstein thought this was ridiculous. He felt perfectly safe in Belgium. Guards were sent to watch over him night and day. He didn't make the situation easy for them. Then a friend, also a German intellectual who spoke out against Hitler, was tracked to Czechoslovakia and murdered. For the first time, Einstein actually realized that he was in danger. Friends finally convinced him to leave Europe.

Einstein resigned himself to making his home in Princeton, New Jersey. It was a pretty town. The people who lived there were curious about this man who dressed badly and was absentminded but had somehow changed the way they thought about the universe. Many were surprised to find that he was a gentle man who spoke kindly to children and milkmen and shopkeepers as he walked to his office each day. Einstein was relieved to find that except for the normal courtesies, most people left him alone.

Albert Einstein, in 1934, a year after he settled in the United States.

People who knew him felt that much of the life had gone out of him. It was as if he had fought for so long and lost so many times that he just didn't have the energy to fight anymore.

By now most scientists accepted his General Theory of Relativity, even though many of them didn't really understand it. One of his goals at Princeton was to help them understand. He bought a house at 112 Mercer Street, and Elsa fixed one of the upstairs rooms as an office for him. His office on campus was Room 209 of the Henry Burchard Fine Hall of Mathematics. Einstein settled into a routine of leaving the house at 9:00 A.M. every day except Sunday, walking a mile to Fine Hall, discussing the unified field theory with a colleague until noon, then walking home again. At home each man worked by himself and then compared notes the next day.

At first Einstein talked in German whenever he could. But as his English got better, he felt a little more comfortable with that language.

In Europe Elsa had managed to control the way Einstein dressed at least a little, but here she lost the battle completely. He wore old trousers, soft shoes or sandals, and, depending on the season, a leather jacket or a gray undershirt. Richard Feynman, professor emeritus at the California Institute of Technology, gave this description: "I remember going to his office when I was a student there. The stories about the way he dressed are true. One day I went to his office to ask a question and I looked down and he didn't have socks on. I had heard that he never wore shirts, and he didn't that day. He just had on a jacket buttoned up to his neck.

"Einstein didn't bother to comb his hair and it was quite

wild. I think he was the original hippie; he felt it didn't matter how you look. What mattered was who you were. I remember that as we talked he was soft-spoken, slow, and thoughtful. I liked him."

From time to time Einstein received letters from students around the country. One young boy wrote that he thought it was rude to classify humans as "animals," even though they belong to the animal kingdom. He wanted to know what Einstein thought. Another asked his opinion on interfaith marriages. Still another wanted to know whether scientists pray and if so, what they prayed about. Others asked what career he thought they should train for. Einstein put a lot of thought into answering the letters. When students asked his advice about going into physics, astronomy, or mathematics, he answered with the feeling he had had as a young man. He wrote that it might be better to make a living at a job they knew they could do while using their spare time to work on things for which they had a great passion.

On their first Christmas Eve in Princeton, children came to the Einstein house singing carols. Einstein enjoyed the music but didn't understand when one of the boys asked for a present. The boy explained that people usually gave them a few pennies for their songs. Einstein asked the boys to wait and came back to the door wearing his jacket and a stocking cap. He showed them his violin and said he would accompany them if he could share the pennies they got.

As news of the insanity in Germany—the persecution, the murders—reached Einstein, he seemed to withdraw more and more. There was a large group of Nazis in New York City, and Einstein was advised not to draw attention to himself. He didn't follow this advice. He accepted an

Dr. Albert Einstein and his son Dr. Hans Albert Einstein.

Albert Einstein, with Fiorello LaGuardia, the mayor of New York City.

invitation to play his violin at a public concert. He was officially welcomed as a resident of New Jersey, and he and Elsa dined with President and Mrs. Franklin D. Roosevelt.

Wanting to make the state's famous resident feel welcome, a New Jersey congressman offered to allow Einstein to become a United States citizen without having to wait the usual five years. Einstein thanked the congressman but said he didn't want special treatment. He would wait.

In the fall of 1936, Elsa became ill. Einstein stopped his daily trips to the institute and worked at home so he could be with her. As she lay in bed, he spent hours reading to her and talking about things that interested her. Elsa wrote to a friend that she never knew Albert loved her so much. On December 21 of that year, Elsa Einstein died.

Einstein had built a strong wall around his feelings, but with Elsa gone he was lonely. He asked his son Hans Albert, now a grown man, to visit, perhaps move, to the United States. He was pleased when his son finally brought his family to the United States to live. Elsa's daughter, Einstein's stepdaughter, Margot, already shared the Mercer Street house, and later his sister, Maja, moved in. Helen Dukas had been living there all along, and she stayed on.

Meanwhile in Europe, Lise Meitner, an Austrian physicist who had been a student of Einstein's in Germany, had been working with others on experiments to break down the uranium atom. She was sure it was possible to release this energy. She conducted the experiments in Germany in 1938. On January 16, 1939, she sent a telegram to Niels Bohr, the greatest atomic physicist in the world. Lise had used Einstein's equation $E = mc^2$ to measure the release of nuclear energy after splitting a uranium atom into two pieces. If she had been able to split enough atoms—all at the same time—

Albert Einstein taking the oath of United States citizenship with his stepdaughter, Margot, right, and his secretary, Helen Dukas. They became American citizens in 1940.

she could have flattened a city. (Similar experiments had been performed earlier by Enrico Fermi in Italy and by Irene and Frederic Joliot-Curie in France.)

This discovery could have belonged to the Germans, and they would have found it very helpful later on. Unfortunately for them, Lise had escaped to Sweden in 1938 after learning that the Gestapo (the Nazi secret police) was planning to take her to one of their infamous concentration camps.

After Bohr received Meitner's telegram, he began work to confirm her theory. Then he rushed to Princeton to talk to Einstein. Over a cup of tea in Einstein's home office, Bohr speculated that if a controlled chain reaction of uranium atom explosions could be set up, scientists might be able to harness atomic energy to make bombs.

Later that year, Germany invaded Poland. Britain and France then declared war on Germany. World War II had begun.

Einstein wasn't convinced that Meitner's theory would work, but he saw that it was possible. Other scientists were easier to convince. Laboratories all over the world began to do tests.

In the spring of 1939, the scientist who led the research in the United States told the U.S. Navy that an atom bomb was a "bare possibility." But what was a bare possibility for the United States was also possible for the Germans. If a bomb so powerful could be made, it had to be the United States, not Germany, that invented it first. Several scientists were convinced that research had to continue. But where would they get the money for this research?

President Franklin D. Roosevelt had to be persuaded to lend his support to the scientists' research efforts. Alexander

Sachs, an unofficial adviser to the president, was approached and agreed. Sachs reasoned that Einstein knew the president, and everyone knew that Einstein stood for peace. If *he* could be persuaded to write a letter to President Roosevelt, the president would be sure to read it carefully.

Einstein was approached. But the idea of lending any kind of support to building a weapon that could kill thousands of people at one time made him feel ill. Still, he knew the Nazis would build the bomb the minute they figured out how to do so. Meitner's laboratory partner was still in Germany. By now he must know what she knew. How long would it take the Germans to catch up? Uranium was essential to the bomb, and Germany was collecting large amounts of this element. Einstein spent many sleepless nights before he agreed to sign the letter. Then, soon after that, he sent a second letter to President Roosevelt in which he added that the bomb should not be used against populated land.

On October 11, 1939, Sachs gave Roosevelt this letter. The Manhattan Project, as the program was called, was launched. About two billion dollars were spent to develop the atom bomb.

Einstein did nothing to help with the project. That was work for others. Though the project was top secret, he couldn't help noticing that several of the country's most important physicists seemed to drop mysteriously out of sight.

On October 1, 1940, seven years after his arrival in the United States, Albert Einstein took the oath of allegiance and became a citizen of the United States. Fourteen months later, on December 7, 1941, the Japanese attacked Pearl Harbor in Hawaii. The United States was drawn into the war.

CHAPTER

8

The Later Years

For four more years after the attack on Pearl Harbor, World War II raged on. Bombs fell on England, Ireland, Italy, France, and Germany. The troops of the United States and its enemy, Japan, fought in the Pacific region. To Einstein it was all madness. Leaders who could not sit at a table and agree to work for peace could send their countries' young men to fight and die for it. In Germany the military was rounding up Jews and shipping them to concentration camps. By the end of the war, 6 million Jewish men, women, and children had been executed in these camps.

Scientists in the United States raced to develop the atom bomb Einstein had written to President Roosevelt about. The bombs the military already had were able to destroy highways and buildings and sent people running in terror for their lives almost every day. The new bomb, an atom bomb, would create an explosion more powerful and destructive than most people could imagine.

Finally, after years of work, the bomb was ready. The first test of the bomb was scheduled for July 16, 1945, in a remote corner of New Mexico. The plan was for the bomb to be dropped from a steel tower. The area around the tower was cleared for miles. The first observation point was set up six miles away. Ten miles away from the tower, scientists paced nervously as the countdown began.

Minus 20 minutes, minus 19, minus 18...minus 10 minutes, minus 9...minus 8.... At minus 45 seconds a robot mechanism took the controls, and the men moved back to safety. The countdown continued...minus three seconds, then two, then one...

The bomb had been dropped. For a moment nobody watching breathed, nobody moved. There was silence. Then there was a flash of light bigger than anything anyone had ever seen; a roar that was more terrible than anyone had ever heard; a rush of hot air that pushed like a terrible wave against everything in its path. A giant smoky cloud billowed from the ground and continued to rise and spread an ugly stain against the sky. Everything on the ground was totally destroyed.

Although some stories say Einstein knew when the bomb was to be tested and even that he was there himself, he did not know officially and he definitely was not there. Einstein wasn't terribly worried about whether the test had been successful. During the early days when the bomb was still just a possibility, President Roosevelt had assured him that if the bomb *did* work, it would never need to be used against people. A demonstration on some wasteland would serve as warning of its destructive power.

But Franklin D. Roosevelt had died, and Harry S. Truman was president now. Army chiefs of staff disagreed with Roosevelt's promise, arguing that while a warning demonstration was being planned, people on both sides of the war would continue to fight and die. As these discussions took place, Germany was defeated and Hitler had killed himself. But Japan still fought and announced to the world that it was willing to fight to the death.

President Truman approved the U.S. Army's request to drop a bomb directly on the enemy, Japan. On August 6, 1945, an American aircraft dropped an atom bomb on the city of Hiroshima. Three days later, another bomb was dropped, this time on the city of Nagasaki. The world was stunned. Within a matter of seconds, more than 120,000 Japanese men, women, and children had died.

Einstein felt betrayed, and his heart ached for the innocent people who had been killed. He blamed himself for their death, feeling that he had been wrong to sign the letter to President Roosevelt. Friends reminded him that if the United States hadn't developed the atom bomb, Germany most certainly would have. And life with Nazi Germany as ruler of the world would have been unbearable. Some of his friends believed that if the bomb had not been dropped on Japan, Japan's soldiers would have fought until there was an even higher death toll.

In spite of the fact that it never seemed to do much good, Einstein threw himself back into his work for peace and became the chairman of the Emergency Committee of Atomic Scientists. Their goal was to encourage nations to share the responsibility of atomic energy and work for peace.

In 1945, at the age of 65, Einstein retired from the Institute for Advanced Study. He still went there daily. He was still driven to find a new theory that would explain both gravity and the electromagnetic field in one set of equations.

In 1947, he began to suffer from terrible stomach pains. He had suffered from bouts of pain, nausea, and vomiting since his illness in 1917. But this time it was worse, and it didn't go away. He grew very weak. Doctors decided to operate. He seemed to be better for a while, then a few years later doctors convinced him that another operation was necessary. This time they found an aneurysm, a small ballooning of a weak wall in an artery in his heart. An examination a few years later showed the condition was getting worse.

Doctors told Einstein he had to slow down and take better care of his health. They forbade him to smoke, but sometimes friends smuggled tobacco past the watchful eyes of Helen Dukas. He was supposed to take it easy, but he continued to go sailing on the campus lake in an old wooden dingy he had bought secondhand.

For years Einstein had felt that his brain was slowing down, but others disagreed. He continued to put in several hours' work every day at the institute. Yet proof of his unified field theory continued to escape him. Even though he was old and frail, he had not lost his appeal to his fans. Often as he walked home, families would stop him and ask if he would pose with them for a picture. He always did.

In 1948 Einstein's first wife, Mileva, died. Mileva had never talked to others much about her husband. But Hans Albert believed he understood his parents' relationship. He believed Einstein had loved her and his sons, but with family around he had just not been able to do his work.

Einstein's sister, Maja, who had gone to Princeton to live just before the war, suffered a paralyzing stroke. For five years, he spent hours every day reading to her. Even after she lapsed into a coma, he continued to read. He felt she might still hear him. When she died in December 1951, Einstein felt as if a part of him also died.

In November 1952, Chaim Weizmann died. This was the man Einstein had traveled throughout the United States with on a fund-raising trip and the man who was the first president of the new state of Israel. Einstein was asked to be the next president of Israel. He was flattered. He had strong feelings about Israel as the Jewish homeland, but he gently declined the offer. The unified field theory that he had been working on in between his work for peace wasn't finished and it had to come first.

In 1955, friends noticed that Einstein had suddenly aged. His legs were so weak that walking to the university seemed difficult. Other parts of his body still appeared solid, but his face had deep lines and looked tired and sad. His hair was absolutely white and the twinkle seemed to be gone from his eyes. His fingers were so weak that he couldn't play the violin.

Einstein knew his time was running out, and the only thing that bothered him was that he hadn't been able to develop the unified field theory. After so many years of trying, it looked as if he wouldn't. He began to suffer from severe stomach pains again. In April, the pains became so bad that doctors wanted to operate immediately. He refused. He was too busy working on a public declaration that would be signed by several of the top scientists, warning of the danger of the nuclear arms race. Besides, he had always felt that everyone has to die sometime, and it wasn't all that important when this happened.

On April 13, he collapsed. Helen Dukas called the

doctor, and a bed was set up in Einstein's study. The following day a specialist from New York arrived and wanted to operate. He said there was a 50-50 chance he might succeed in repairing the artery. Einstein had already made his views on death known, and he refused. The following day, he seemed improved, but the day after that he was in such pain he was unable to move. Doctors insisted on taking him to the hospital.

There was time for visits by his stepdaughter Margot and by Hans Albert. Shortly after midnight on April 18, 1955, the weak artery broke and Albert Einstein died. He was 76 years old.

He had not been able to find a solution to the problem he had been working on for years. But he had done more than any other man in physics had done.

The scientist Richard Feynman said: "Whenever any great discovery is made in physics you look at it and say—It's so *obvious*, why didn't *I* think of that? Why didn't others? But that wasn't true with Einstein's General Theory of Relativity. It wasn't an obvious theory; it took dramatically deep analysis. I would have never gotten that idea. I can't think of anyone else who would have either."

Einstein had left instructions on what was to be done when he died. He said there was to be no funeral, no grave, and no monument. His brain could be used for research, he said, but he wanted to be cremated. His wishes were carried out exactly. He was cremated and a friend took the ashes to a nearby river and scattered them there.

With his family's approval, Einstein's brain was removed during the autopsy and carefully examined under a microscope. Although nothing about this examination has ever been published, it is known that doctors found nothing

Albert Einstein in 1954 on his seventy-fifth birthday.

unusual in the brain's size, weight, or formation. It was just what one would expect for a man who was 76 years old.

Albert Einstein may be one of the most written-about people in modern history, yet few people really knew the man. From the beginning he believed his personal life, his private thoughts and feelings, were no one's business but his own. When reporters asked intruding questions, he refused to answer.

He was known as an absentminded scientist who couldn't even remember his own telephone number. In truth, he was absentminded only about things that didn't matter to him or about things he knew someone else would remember for him. When it came to important matters, like physics, his memory was quite good.

Some who knew Albert Einstein felt sorry for him. They felt that his physics took so much thought that he didn't have time to enjoy life as they did. It was true. He lived a pretty Spartan and isolated life, but he had no regrets about that. He had *chosen* to live his life in that way.

If he did have any regrets, it was that his son Eduard would have to spend the rest of his life in a mental sanatorium and that he himself had been unable to prove his unified field theory. Actually, there were very few men in the world who would even have been qualifed to *work* on the subject.

Einstein never tried to win honors or awards, and he couldn't understand why people gave them to him just for doing physics. But for nearly half a century, honors and awards *were* bestowed on him. The world knew what a special man he was and refused to let him go unnoticed.

Important Dates

1879 Albert Einstein is born on March 14 in Ulm, Germany, the son of Hermann and Pauline Einstein.

1884 Albert Einstein, a young Jewish boy, enters a Catholic elementary school in Munich, a city to which the Einstein family had moved in 1881.

1889 Einstein enters the Luitpold Gymnasium, a secondary school.

1895 Einstein fails the entrance examination to the Swiss Federal Polytechnic School in Zürich, Switzerland.

1896 Einstein enters the Swiss Federal Polytechnic School in Zürich where he studies until his graduation in 1900.

1900 Einstein's first physics research paper is published in *Annalen der Physik,* a German physics magazine.

1901 Einstein becomes a Swiss citizen.

1902 Einstein begins work at the Swiss Patent Office in Bern and works there until 1909.

1903 Einstein marries Mileva Maric.

1905 Einstein has several important scientific papers published, including the one that presents his Special Theory of Relativity.

1908 Einstein accepts an offer of a teaching position as a lecturer at the University of Bern.

1909 Einstein accepts a position as associate professor of theoretical physics at the University of Zürich and moves with his family back to Zürich.

1911 Einstein accepts a position as a professor of experimental physics at the German University in Prague, Czechoslovakia, and moves with his family to Prague.

1912 Einstein accepts a position as full professor at the Swiss Federal Polytechnic School in Zürich, Switzerland.

1914 Einstein returns to Germany with his family. They live in Berlin where Einstein heads the Kaiser Wilhelm Physical Institute, is a professor at the University of Berlin, and becomes a member of the Royal Prussian Academy of Sciences.

1914 Mileva returns to Switzerland with her two sons.

1914–1918 World War I. Einstein opposes the war.

1915 Einstein develops his General Theory of Relativity.

1916 Einstein publishes the paper presenting his General Theory of Relativity.

1919 London's Royal Astronomical Society observes a rare eclipse of the sun. Their experiments prove that Einstein's theories about gravitation are correct. Einstein divorces Mileva. and marries Elsa.

1921 Einstein and Elsa sail to the United States, where as a Zionist, Einstein tours the country raising money for Hebrew University, which Jews were building in their homeland in Palestine.

1922 Einstein receives the 1921 Nobel Prize in physics.

1929 Einstein publishes a paper dealing with his proposed unified field theory.

1931 Einstein and Elsa travel to Pasadena, California, where he accepts the first of several short lecture appointments at the California Institute of Technology.

1932 Einstein speaks to representatives from 60 nations at a meeting in Switzerland at which he urges each country to establish laws to prevent nations from attacking each other.

1933 Nazi threats against Einstein's life convince him to leave Germany permanently. He accepts an appointment at the Institute for Advanced Study in Princeton, New Jersey.

1939–1945 World War II.

1939 Einstein sends a letter to President Franklin D. Roosevelt urging him to provide scientists with money to develop an atomic bomb before Nazi Germany does.

1940 Einstein becomes a citizen of the United States.

1945 The United States drops two atomic bombs on Japan.

1952 Einstein is asked to become president of Israel but declines the offer.

1955 Albert Einstein, age 76, dies on April 18.

Bibliography

Beckhard, Arthur. *Albert Einstein*. New York: G. P. Putnam's Sons, 1959.

Bernstein, Jeremy. *Einstein*. New York: The Viking Press, 1973.

Clark, Ronald W. *Einstein, The Life and Times*. New York: A Discus Book/Published by Avon Books, 1972.

Cuny, Hilaire. *Albert Einstein, The Man and His Theories*. Middlebury, Vt.: Paul S. Eriksson, Inc., 1965.

Dank, Milton. *Albert Einstein*. New York: Franklin Watts, 1983.

Dukas, Helen, and Hoffman, Banesh, eds. *Albert Einstein, The Human Side*. Princeton, N.J.: Princeton University Press, 1979.

Dupuy, Col. T. N. *A Genius for War: The General Staff 1897–1945*. Englewood Cliffs, New Jersey: Prentice Hall, 1977.

Levinger, Elma Ehrlich. *Albert Einstein*. New York: Messner, 1949.

Michelmore, Peter. *Einstein, Profile of the Man*. New York: Dodd, Mead & Co., 1962.

Schwartz, Joseph, and McGuinness, Michael. *Einstein for Beginners*. New York: Pantheon Books, 1979.

Index

About the Author

Karin Ireland has written four books for children and two humor books for adults. She also works as a writer for a large corporation in Irvine, California. Ms. Ireland lives in Newport Beach, California, with her daughter, Tricia.